Karla and Grif

a play in two acts

by

Vivienne Laxdal

Playwrights Canada Press
Toronto • Canada

We acknowledge the support of The Canada Council for the
Arts for our publishing programme, and the Ontario Arts
Council.

*Cover art: c.j. fleury, graphics by Creative Minds. Image based on
the National Arts Centre production poster featuring Brooke
Johnson and Cary Lawrence as photographed by Gordon King.
Playwright photo by Marcel Chevassu.*

Canadian Cataloguing in Publication Data
Laxdal, Vivienne,
    Karla and Grif
A play
ISBN 0-88754-570-X
I. Title.
PS8573.A945K37 1999   C812.54   C99-93106203
PR9199.3.L336K37 1999

First edition: November 1999.
Printed and bound by Hignell Printing, Winnipeg, Canada.

The playwright gratefully acknowledges the support and assistance in the development of this play from the following: Barbara Lysnes, Theatre B.C.; Dorothy Ward, The National Arts Centre; Tarragon Theatre; Centaur Theatre; Urjo Kareda, John Palmer, and the casts of the first two productions.

Beginning her career as an actress, Vivienne turned to writing plays about the same time she started having kids. Now she now does it all — and pumps iron, too. She lives in the woods in West Quebec, but often crosses the border to have her work produced. Ottawa audiences have attended premiere productions of her work at The Great Canadian Theatre Company and The National Arts Centre. Her works for the stage have been produced across Canada and in San Francisco. CBC Radio has broadcast a number of her radio dramas.

Her plays for adult audiences include "Cyber:\womb", "National Capitale Nationale" (directed by Robert Lepage), "Personal Convictions", "Karla and Grif", and "Goose Spit". In 1995, she was awarded the Ottawa Valley Book Festival - Dave Smith Playwriting Award for "Cyber:\womb" (recently published by Blizzard Press in *Prerogatives: Contemporary Plays by Women*). Other awards and prizes include the CBC Radio Drama Competition, a Canadian Authors Association Award, and first place in the Canadian National Playwriting Competition for "Karla and Grif".

She has been resident playwright at The Centaur Theatre in Montreal, and an invited member of the Playwrights Units at The Great Canadian Theatre Company, The Canadian Stage Company (Toronto) and Odyssey Theatre (Ottawa).

Vivienne has performed many of her own pieces for voice and stage, and has taken part in several readings, workshops and theatre events around Ottawa. She has written and performed her own commentaries for CBC television, and has twice guest-appeared on CBC Newsday's "Pop-Culture Panel."

Recent acting credits include the role of Marie Ange in Michel Trembley's "Les Belles Soeurs", directed by Micheline Chevrier (1997); and the role of Angela in Michael Ondaatje's "The Collected Works of Billy The Kid", directed by Richard Rose (1998), both at The Great Canadian Theatre Company.

INTRODUCTION

When I was 14 years old my mother had her seventh and final child. She was 42. Like me, she is small and each day she would spend at least an hour with her beautiful baby, my brother, cooing and cuddling in the tiny rocking chair that sat in the corner of the kitchen. I quite adored my new bro Matthew but I must admit that even at 14 I was a bit envious of the time my mother spent with him. By that age my personality was made up of that fabulous adolescent combination of continual criticism, childish impertinence and presumed arrogance. I will never forget the day I found my mother's display of affection toward my brother embarrassingly solipsistic. I pronounced to her that "That baby is gonna love himself." With a very direct and heartfelt response my mother said, "Paula, that is the whole idea."

This incident was a formulating moment in my life. Even through my insolence I could recognize the truth in my mother's words. To love oneself is the whole idea. It is this notion of love that has informed my thinking. One of the greatest struggles of our time is toward love. Since the dawn of the modern age it is through love that we have come to know and define ourselves. Identifying how to give and receive love is an act of fulfillment toward one's self and toward others. It is part of the responsibility of living in a just world.

This is what fascinates me about Karla and Grif. It is a story about two girls who are conscious of the importance of being loved and loving. They have found in each other a friendship that allows them to explore the limitless parameters of intimacy. Through the course of the play they expose themselves to each other in every way and thereby become intricately bonded. It is an evolving course of agreement that brings them to the threshold of trust. Crossing over into each other becomes a total act of faith. By entering this dangerous terrain of mutual expectation they consciously risk losing themselves to the prospect of being loved. It is a high stakes maneuvre in the lives of these adolescents and has enormous consequences for their future.

Karla and Grif are young women who have never been nurtured. One has been abandoned by her mother and left to parent her father, the other has lost both parents and is bound to the subscribed world of her grandmother. The beauty of these characters is that, despite the deprivations of their pasts, they insist on absolute honesty and integrity in the present. The pain in the relationship comes with the realization that self worth cannot be dependant on a reflection from others. They can not cultivate each other until they can nourish themselves. They use each other to learn to love and in the process experience the pain of coming to know themselves.

It is a familiar struggle. The complexity of the drama is how Vivienne reveals basic needs through extraordinary circumstances. She can turn an act of desperation into a moment of recognition. Despite the cruelty of their actions, Karla and Grif inspire compassion. They extract from each other an exchange that can hardly be considered healthy. There is no living happily ever after in this play. Vivienne doesn't settle for stasis, she pushes for evolution. In "Karal and Grif" she addresses an ongoing pursuit which brings adolescent girls from a nascent state to the possibility of mature love.

Paula Danckert
Playwrights' Workshop Montreal, 1999

PRODUCTION HISTORY

"Karla and Grif" was first produced in March of 1991 by the National Arts Centre English Theatre as part of the Atelier Workshop Programme.

KARLA	*Brooke Johnson*
GRIF	*Cary Lawrence*
DANNY	*David Fox*
KATHY	*Sarah Snow*

Director - Barbara Lysnes.
Dramaturge - Urjo Kareda.
Set/Costumes by James Cameron.
Lighting by Gerry Van Hezewyk.
Music/Sound by Ian Tamblyn.

"Karla and Grif" was subsequently produced by The Centaur Theatre, Montreal, February, 1992.

KARLA	*Brooke Johnson*
GRIF	*Catherine MacKenzie*
KATHY	*Rebecca Dewey*
DANNY	*Dean Hawes*

Director - John Palmer.
Set/Costumes by James Cameron.
Lights - Don Finlayson
Music/Sound by Ian Tamblyn.

FURTHER PRODUCTIONS
• Theatre Rhinoceros - directed by Adele Prandini, San Francisco, 1995
• Sea Theatre - directed by Bill Devine, Vancouver 1996

CHARACTERS

KARLA - early 20's.
GRIF - early 20's.
DANNY - late 40's.
KATHY - 30 something.

SETTINGS

• Apartment Corridor.
• Interior of Grif's bachelor apartment on the market: kitchen counter, couch and window necessary.
• Interior of a summer residence camp staff cabin for two: bunk beds, wooden spring-hinge door.
• Danny's living room: 'lazy-boy' chair, side table.

Note: These settings need only be suggested in design. Easy on-stage access is necessary to each setting.

TIME

The scenes that originate in Grif's apartment take place in October, 1991.
Summer camp scenes and Danny's living room scenes are scattered throughout the past without particular respect to chronological time.

PRODUCTION NOTE

This play is presented from Karla's point of view — or from her mind's eye. Often a scene from her past will intrude upon her present — sometimes bursting on in bits, other times creeping up slowly to result in complete scenes. Occasionally, they occur simultaneously with the present. Karla may be pulled directly into a scene from the past, or it might be played within the setting she is in at the time. For this reason, there is no numbered breakdown of scenes in the text per se, as they often mingle — and never is there a need for a complete blackout (except at the end of Act One). Effective lighting design should emphasise where Karla's attention is directed.

The part of the set being used, i.e. The Cabin, or The Apartment, is indicated in the preceding stage direction.

Act One

Apartment Corridor.
KARLA stands smoking beside a closed door.
She lets the ashes drop to the floor.

SOUND: Wooden spring door slamming.
Cabin.

GRIF   (*offstage*) Karla! Karla!

         GRIF appears at camp door and speaks
         directly to KARLA.

I'm here!

         SOUND: Metal door slamming.
         Danny's Place.
         DANNY is seated in his chair. He speaks
         directly to KARLA.

DANNY   Hey! Hey! When the hell did you get back?

GRIF   Did you miss me? Did you miss me?

DANNY   Why didn't you call me? I would have come
         and got you.

GRIF   How are you!? Kiss kiss kiss kiss kiss!

DANNY   Oh, my baby girl. All tanned and beautiful.
         Let me look at you.

GRIF   Holy Christ! You got a—

DANNY   Hey, uh ... how's your—

GRIF   What happened?

DANNY   Stupid accident.

GRIF   You don't want to tell me.

DANNY   It's going to change. I mean it.

GRIF   Twenty questions!

DANNY   Hey, where you going?

GRIF   We are going to have the best summer!

              GRIF runs out the door.

DANNY   Don't you want to talk to me? Karla? Eh!?

              Corridor.
              *Upon the sound of someone approaching,
              KARLA drops her cigarette and extinguishes it
              with her foot. GRIF hurriedly enters, carrying
              a bag of groceries, a bag from a lingerie
              boutique, an umbrella and a briefcase. She
              doesn't notice KARLA at first as she is
              fumbling in her briefcase for her keys. Her
              umbrella drops. She stoops to pick it up.*

KARLA   Hi, Grif.

GRIF   (*shocked motionless*) Karla!

KARLA   Still raining? Here.

              *KARLA takes the umbrella and opens and
              shuts it quickly to shake off the water.*

GRIF   That's okay, I can—

KARLA   You look good. What did you do to your hair?

GRIF   What? I didn't... Nothing.

KARLA   It's lighter or something.

GRIF   How long have you been here?

KARLA   I think I liked it the other way, better.

GRIF   How did you find my apartment?

KARLA   Dirty blonde. Or sandy brown. Sort of.

GRIF   Did you ... you didn't call my grandmother, did you?

KARLA   I don't know. Maybe I just remember it different.

GRIF   She, she isn't well. She shouldn't have any stress. Her heart—

KARLA   Did you know they put addresses in phone books?

                 Pause.

GRIF   I didn't think you lived here anymore.

KARLA   Why?

GRIF   I'm in a bit of a rush.

KARLA   I love this city.

GRIF   I have to be somewhere at 7:00.

KARLA   Dinner date?

                 Pause.

GRIF   Karla, I wasn't expecting... If I'd known—

KARLA   I wanted to surprise you. Surprise!

GRIF   We could have arranged something. I don't really have time—

KARLA   Just a quick visit. Shoot the shit. Cup of coffee. Here, give me something.

GRIF   You should have phoned.

KARLA   I did. I just kept getting your machine. I can't stand those things. You've been out a lot. Here, let me help you.

> *KARLA reaches out to take something from GRIF. GRIF doesn't move.*

KARLA   Are we going in, or what?

GRIF   Karla—

KARLA   What's the matter? You hiding something in there?

Oh, wait. Is there a man in there? Waiting for you in a muscle shirt and bikini briefs? Trained to kill uninvited guests?

GRIF   No, I... Why don't you just tell me what you want?

KARLA   To see you. Talk to you. It's been over three years. Three years ... and a couple of months, maybe.

GRIF   I just don't think this is—

KARLA   Open the friggin' door!

GRIF   I'm sorry. I'm busy. I'm going out.

KARLA   You don't have to be there 'til seven.

GRIF   I need a shower.

KARLA   That still gives us a few minutes...

GRIF   I have nothing to say to you.

KARLA   Okay, open the door or I'll yell something obscene. In five...

GRIF   What?

KARLA   Four...

GRIF   What, you're not going to yell in here.

KARLA   The old lady across the hall came home ten
               minutes ago. Three...

GRIF   No Karla, you can't be serious.

KARLA   You're running out of time. Two...

GRIF   Oh, come on!

KARLA   That's the rule. One...

GRIF   Jesus, Karla!

KARLA   (*hollering*) JANET GRIFFITHS HAS RED
               PUBIC HAIR!

               GRIF quickly turns and starts to walk away.
               KARLA grabs her arm.

KARLA   Hey. I could have yelled about the time you
               shaved it all off.

GRIF   What do you want, Karla?

               Pause.

KARLA   Danny died.

GRIF   Really?

KARLA   No. I'm lying.

GRIF   I'm sorry.

KARLA   Want to see his obituary? I brought it for you.
               In case you missed it in the papers.

               GRIF doesn't take it.

KARLA   Actually, it wasn't in the big paper, or anything. I'm not the obituary-writing type. It was in the company newsletter.

GRIF   You could have just told me this first instead of going through all the bullshit.

KARLA   (*mock terror*) You swore!

GRIF   Are you on drugs, Karla?

     KARLA laughs.

GRIF   Are you?

KARLA   Good ol' Janet.

     Pause.

No, Grif. I'm straight. I'm clean. I'm dry. I haven't dropped a speck for three years.

Now, doesn't that beat all to hell? Unless you count cigarettes and the occasional beer.

     Pause.

What, no confetti? No streamers?

GRIF   That's very good.

KARLA   No hugs?

     Pause.

So, how about it? Gonna let me in?

     Pause.

GRIF   (*punctuating*) I have to leave in half an hour.

KARLA   That doesn't give us much, does it?

GRIF   Half an hour.

KARLA   I'll take what I can get.

GRIF   A cup of coffee.

> *KARLA offers to take some of the load. GRIF hesitates, then hands her the groceries. She finds her keys in her pocket and opens the door.*

KARLA   Ladies first.

> *GRIF goes through the door.*

> **Danny's Place.**
> *DANNY swivels his chair around to face KARLA.*

DANNY   I think you ought to wear a dress.

> *KARLA approaches him.*

KARLA   When was the last time you saw me wear a dress, Danny?

> *DANNY thinks.*

                 Right.

DANNY   It's just... It's sort of formal.

KARLA   (*guffaws*) Formal.

DANNY   Yeah. Formal.

KARLA   Schmitke's Tool and Dye Company has a "formal" Christmas party?

DANNY   So what's wrong with that, Karla? Eh? What's wrong with people putting on decent clothes once in a while?

> *KARLA smirks.*

DANNY   What? What?

KARLA   Nothing.

DANNY   You know, it wouldn't hurt you, Karla. To make yourself more...

KARLA   What?

DANNY   You could be a real looker, you know. Lots of guys would think you'd be a real catch.

KARLA   I'm not a muskie for Chrissake.

DANNY   A little bit of rouge, earrings maybe—

KARLA   I suppose you'd want me to clean under my fucking fingernails, too.

DANNY   Hey, hey!

KARLA   Look, you want me to go with you, I said I'd go. You want a dress, find a date.

DANNY   Aw, c'mon Karla...

KARLA   And anyway, what are you going to wear? You don't even have a jacket.

> **The Cabin.**
> *GRIF enters with a 'majestic' air, capturing KARLA's attention. DANNY continues speaking to KARLA.*

GRIF   You should have seen us at the grad, Karla. We were a vision.

DANNY   Well, forget it then.

GRIF   An absolute vision!

DANNY   We won't go.

GRIF   Gram took me to this little German boutique.

DANNY   I'll be sick or something.

GRIF   They made such a fuss. Opalescent satin. Off-
         the-shoulder puff. Deep V in the back. Floor-
         length skirt...

DANNY   I just thought it would be fun for us.

GRIF   ...Like Cinderella!

DANNY   Do something special.

GRIF   It took me hours to get dressed. It took Al
         thirty seconds to rip it off. Want to see the
         picture?

              GRIF exits.

DANNY   When was the last time we went out together,
         eh? Can you even remember? I remember. It
         was last summer. After you came back from
         camp. We had steak. I let you have some
         wine, too. You were underage. To celebrate your
         bronze cross.

KARLA   (*frustrated*) Bronze medallion Danny!

              She turns away from him.

         It was my bronze medallion!

              KARLA exits.

DANNY   (*yells after her*) I was real proud of you for that,
         Karla! Real proud! That camp was a good
         place for you. I knew that. A place to learn
         something good. Get out of the city. Get away
         from those degenerates you called your friends!

         Healthy air. Clean water. Sun. Exercise...

The Cabin.
*KARLA enters the cabin with her bedroll,
backpack and boom box. She has a cast on her
fore arm.*

DANNY ... knee socks, running shoes, tee shirts and
shorts.

And girls!

Lots of girls your own age, Karla. It'll be fun!

That's what my little girl needs.

*KARLA dumps her gear. She slaps the bunk
mattress. Dust clouds upward. On her hands
and knees she checks under the bed. She scans
the walls looking for the past year's
signatures.*

GRIF *(off)* KARLA! KARLA! I'M HERE!

*KARLA quickly assumes a nonchalant
position on the bottom bunk, hiding her cast.
GRIF enters with a flourish. On her T-shirt is
printed: "CAMP CEDAR ROCK - GRIF -
SENIOR WATERFRONT" She drops her
gear.*

GRIF *(almost without taking a breath)* AAAAAHHH!
LOOK AT YOU! Kiss kiss kiss kiss kiss. Did
you miss me? DID YOU MISS ME?
Congratulate me, you are looking at a survivor
of first year psychology. OH, GOD, I'M SO
GLAD TO BE UP HERE! PRE-CAMP PARTY!
WOO-HOO! I had to do some sweet-talking to
get Boss Lady to let us share a cabin again, you
know. I promised her no late night raids in the
tuck cupboard. Hey, did you see the new bell
on the mess hall? How the hell are we going
to steal the gonger when it's on top of the roof?
I'll bet you Boss Lady did that. BIIITCH! Oh,
man! Look at this place! It's so clean! I wonder
if "Mr. T"'s still alive.

She bangs on the bottom bunk and peers under it.

COME ON OUT YOU ROTTEN RODENT! Bet he's got a whole nest of them under here. Little "Mr. T"'s to scare the shit out of us at night. Hey, you little bugger! Better watch it or Big Bad Karla will get you with her knife. (*to KARLA*) You still got the Sabre?

KARLA takes her beaten, old pocket knife out of her pocket.

All right! "Camper Threatening Device". Remember last year, when we were on night duty, we scared the pants off of cabin Ten. I've never seen a more still bunch of thirteen-year-olds in my life. God that was funny! They're sitting there, having a seance in the middle of the floor and in slams Grif and Karla with the SABRE! You were so funny, Karla... standing there, your knife glistening in the spot of my flashlight, a wild glare in your eyes. God, if Boss Lady had ever found out about that we would have been fired for sure. HOLY CHRIST! YOU GOT A BROKEN ARM!

KARLA   Swift.

GRIF   AAAAHH! SHE TALKS!

KARLA   When I have a chance.

            KARLA sticks her knife into the bunk post.

GRIF   So, how'd you break it?

KARLA   You want the top?

GRIF   Karla, we've been coming to Cedar Rock for eight years. I've always had the top bunk.

KARLA   So, do you want it again?

GRIF   Why? Do you want it?

KARLA   I was being polite.

GRIF   Well, you already got your stuff on the bottom.

KARLA   It's not unpacked.

GRIF   And how would you climb up there with a broken arm?

KARLA   No problem.

GRIF   Piss off. I want the top. Oh, you forgot to pick up your tee shirt at the office.

> *GRIF throws KARLA's staff tee shirt to her. KARLA holds it up against herself. It reads "CAMP CEDAR ROCK - KITCHEN - KARLA."*

GRIF   Well, put it on!

KARLA   Later.

> *They start to unpack their bedrolls.*

GRIF   So, what fine items are on the menu for our gourmet campers this summer, hm? More chicken-a-la-shit?

KARLA   Tuna casserole with puss sauce.

GRIF   All you can eat Road-Kill Meat!

KARLA   And Grif's personal favourite:

BOTH   Phlegm flambé!

> *They simultaneously pretend hork and spit.*

KARLA   There it is!

GRIF screeches and leaps onto the bunk,
frantically checking the floor.

GRIF   Where!

KARLA   No, bone head, "Grif and Karla, 1987".

GRIF   Don't do that!

KARLA   Wimp.

GRIF   We are going to have the best summer.

KARLA   Right on.

GRIF   So, are you going to tell me what happened?

KARLA   My father broke it.

GRIF   Your father.

KARLA   Yup.

GRIF   Your father broke your arm.

KARLA   You got it.

GRIF   Karla!

KARLA   What?

GRIF   You don't just stand there calmly, and calmly
        tell me your father broke your arm!

KARLA   What do you want me to do? Cry? It doesn't
        hurt anymore.

GRIF   How did it happen?

KARLA   How's your grandmother?

GRIF   No. Don't change the subject.

KARLA   She still have that Caribbean cook?

GRIF   You don't want to tell me.

KARLA   The one with the "nice" buns?

GRIF   Okay. "20 Questions."

KARLA   Does he still make "Miss Janet" her favourite
              "sugar sweets"?

GRIF   Was it an accident?

KARLA   And teach you how to "play his drums"?

GRIF   Was it an accident?

KARLA   (*sighs*) No.

GRIF   Were you fighting?

KARLA   Yes.

GRIF   About your mother?

KARLA   No.

GRIF   About your friends?

KARLA   No.

GRIF   About school?

KARLA   Well, in a way...

GRIF   No, no! You can only answer "yes" or "no"!

KARLA   Yes.

GRIF   Yes. Okay. Wait a minute, I lost count. Did I
              have five or six?

KARLA   Fuck this.

GRIF   Oh. By the way. I'm making a rule for us for
              this summer.

KARLA	Who died and left you in charge?
GRIF	No swearing allowed.
KARLA	In front of the kids.
GRIF	No. At all.
KARLA	So what are we supposed to say instead of shit, fuck or piss?
GRIF	Hey, hey!
KARLA	Well?
GRIF	Piffle.
KARLA	Piffle?
GRIF	Piffle.
KARLA	Stupidest word I ever heard.
GRIF	That's the rule.
KARLA	And what happens if we break it?
GRIF	You get spanked.
KARLA	What happens if you like spankings?
GRIF	You would. So, tell me about your fight.
KARLA	Well, I got booted from school—
GRIF	Again?
KARLA	Took too many classes off.
GRIF	Karla.
KARLA	I called the vice principal an asshole—
GRIF	You did?

KARLA   He caught me and Spider sharing a splif under the football stands.

GRIF   You're still doing that stuff?

KARLA   He said I was to keep my feet off school property until I "straightened" my ways. I said, "You got it, asshole!"

GRIF   Cripes!

KARLA   So, I went home. And I'd just broke into my Dad's new case of Brador... He's really protective of his Brador... If it's 50 or Canadian he really doesn't give a shit—

GRIF   Hey—

KARLA   But touch his Brador and you're up SHIT creek!

GRIF   (*warning*) Karla!

KARLA   Then, Danny walks in. He's as red as a lobster. The principal called him at work. So, he tells his boss he has a family emergency and he has to get home immediately.

GRIF   Oh, man.

KARLA   He walks in ... and I'm standing there, drinking his precious Brador. He starts yelling that I should buy my own beer. I tell him to take a hike, and I try to finish the beer. Then he grabs my arm, and smashes it on the door frame.

GRIF   Oh, shit!

KARLA   Ha!

GRIF   Piffle! Piffle! I mean piffle!

> *KARLA raises her hand, and tries to corner GRIF.*

KARLA   Bend over!

GRIF   No, no!

KARLA   Pull your pants down!

GRIF   Not with pants down!

KARLA   That's what a spanking is.

GRIF   My grandmother never spanked me.

KARLA   She should have.

GRIF   Come on, Karla. It was a joke.

> *KARLA drops her hand.*

KARLA   Next time, I pull out the wooden spoon. Or, no, the kitchen paddle — the one I use for stirring the oatmeal.

GRIF   Alright, alright!

KARLA   I mean it.

GRIF   Okay! So, he smashed your arm on the door frame?

KARLA   The bottle flies out of my hand and smashes right through the window.

GRIF   Jeepers. And your arm's broken.

KARLA   Thin little bones there, you know. You should have heard it.

GRIF   Gawd!

KARLA   Cast comes off next week.

GRIF   (*sympathetic*) Oh, Karla.

KARLA   (*mimicking*) Oh, Grif.

> *GRIF tries to hug KARLA. KARLA squirms away.*

KARLA   Stop it.

GRIF   What are you going to do about it?

KARLA   Oh, I'm going to sue him. Or maybe, I'll report him to Children's Aid. Except I'm eighteen now.

GRIF   I'm serious. You should—

KARLA   I should what?

GRIF   He should pay for that.

KARLA   Well, I'm on his medical card.

GRIF   He can't just go around breaking your arm like that, Karla.

KARLA   I'm the one who fucked up, Grif. And I don't give a shit about your stupid rule at the moment.

GRIF   What about the police?

KARLA   He's my father!

GRIF   He broke your arm!

KARLA   And I drank his beer, and failed another year!

GRIF   Boy, if my father ever...

KARLA   Your father's dead, Grif.

GRIF   Or my grandmother, then!

KARLA smirks.

GRIF   This isn't funny! I can't believe he did that to you. Over a stupid beer!

KARLA   He didn't mean to break it!

GRIF   What exactly did he mean to do, then?

KARLA   It doesn't matter!

GRIF   He shouldn't be...

KARLA   Let's just drop it, okay?

        KARLA abruptly turns and leaves the cabin.

GRIF   Karla!

        SOUND: House door slamming.

        Danny's Place.
        DANNY is watching late-night television. On the side table beside his chair, there is a half-eaten, store-bought freezer cake, an empty pack of cigarettes, and a bottle of Brador.

DANNY   That you, Karla?

        KARLA enters.

KARLA   No. It's Freddy Krueger.

        KARLA stands behind DANNY watching the television. She picks up the bottle and takes a swig. DANNY takes the beer from her without looking away from the TV.

DANNY   There's Canadian in the basement.

KARLA   Want a cigarette?

DANNY   Eh?

KARLA   Your pack's empty. Here.

             She hands him a cigarette. He accepts.

DANNY   There's Brador in the fridge.

             KARLA picks up the cake box.

KARLA   What the hell are you buying this shit for,
             Danny?

DANNY   Watch your language.

KARLA   Look at this crap. You look at what's in here?
             Listen. Sodium aluminum silicate. Triethyl
             citrate. Propylene mono fatty acid esters.
             Sorbitan mono stearate—

DANNY   Shut the fuck up, I can't hear the television.

KARLA   You don't have to eat this garbage. You want a
             cake, ask me. I'll make you a cake.

DANNY   She'll make me a cake.

KARLA   I would.

DANNY   Where you been?

KARLA   What's it matter?

DANNY   It matters 'cause I wanna know.

KARLA   You wanna know when I shit and piss too?

DANNY   She gets defensive on me because I ask her
             where she's been!

KARLA   At the Chaud (*pronounced "shawd"*), okay?

DANNY   With who?

KARLA   Same people I always go with.

DANNY You gotta stop hanging around those goofs, Karla.

KARLA Don't tell me what to do.

DANNY They're no good, Karla.

KARLA Goodnight.

　　　　KARLA moves to exit.

DANNY You know who made good cakes? Joyce made good cakes. Big chocolate ones.

KARLA I remember.

DANNY She remembers. Tell me how the hell you remember when you were only three years old for Chrissake!

KARLA I remember! Big two-layer jobs. And she decorated them with goddamn gumdrops!

DANNY Gummy bears, Karla. Gummy bears. She put gummy bears on them because I liked the contrast. Sweet and sour. She remembers. Hey! You know why you remember? I know why. You don't remember anything. You've seen the pictures.

KARLA No, I remember getting a cake like that on my birthday.

DANNY Jesus! It wasn't your birthday, Karla! It was mine! The one you're remembering was my cake!

KARLA She probably made it more than once, Dan.

DANNY Look. I'll show you the cake you're "remembering" Karla.

　　　　DANNY reaches for a worn photo album from the side table.

KARLA   Forget it.

DANNY   I ought to know what cake Joyce made for me on my birthday. It's right in here.

KARLA   Okay. Alright. You're right. Don't get out the stupid photo album.

DANNY   Don't tell me what to do, Karla. Where the hell's that picture?

KARLA   I'm going to bed.

DANNY   Just get back here, Missy. Here! Look! Here it is! The chocolate cake with the gummy bears. And it's sitting right in front of me.

KARLA   Look at it close, Dad.

DANNY   What?

KARLA   There's three candles on it.

DANNY   So what? Maybe I turned thirty-three and she just shortened it.

KARLA   And I'm sitting there, Danny, with my cheeks all puffed up, like I'm going to blow out the candles!

DANNY   You were always butting in. It was MY cake, and you were trying to blow out MY candles.

KARLA   I don't believe you! It's my birthday cake, on my third birthday. And I remember it without the fucking picture.

DANNY   Shut up, Karla.

KARLA   Look! Look! The next picture. What is it, Dan? It's me. Me opening a present. A present on MY third birthday!

DANNY   You couldn't keep your mitts off anything.
                Everything was "mine, mine, mine." It's my
                birthday present you're opening.

KARLA   The wrapping's got pictures of teddy bears on
                it!

DANNY   Joyce was cheap. She saved wrapping paper.

KARLA   And balloons on the wall!

DANNY   Can it!

KARLA   She put balloons on the wall when you turned
                thirty-three? Eh, Danny? EH!?

DANNY   YOU GONNA SHUT YOUR YAP?!

                *DANNY violently grabs KARLA's arm and
                breaks it. KARLA yells in pain.*

DANNY   Oh, Jesus. Oh, what did I do?

KARLA   It was MY birthday, you BASTARD!

                KARLA exits holding her arm.

DANNY   Oh, Jesus. Oh, Karla...

                *DANNY holds himself and rocks in his
                chair.*

                *KARLA returns to the cabin. She and GRIF
                are silent for a moment.*

                The Cabin.

GRIF   Hey, you know what I heard? Half the
                camper population this session is on Social
                Aid.

                Hey, wanna lay bets on the number of
                runaways? Or no ... let's do suicide attempts.

Yeah. Five bucks on ... seventeen boffed suicide attempts from the social aid population.

Remember that fat girl last summer? Drank two bottles of rubbing alcohol? And that other one? From cabin seven? The one with only one pair of shorts? Tried to slit her wrists with a butter knife?

Only on social assistance.

Pause.

(*ashamed*) Oh, Karla. I'm sorry...

KARLA   No. You're just rich.

GRIF   I'm not rich.

KARLA   A house on Embassy Row isn't exactly middle class, Grif.

GRIF   It's very old money, Karla.

KARLA   Is it too old to spend?

GRIF   Look, I lived in a split-level in Nepean until I was three years old.

KARLA   Life's rough.

GRIF   My parents had to work, you know. They both had jobs. They weren't just handed the family money. That trip they were taking was the first vacation they'd had in four years.

KARLA   I know.

GRIF   My grandmother has been very good to me. I love her. But, I'd rather have my mother and father, you know?

KARLA   Okay!

GRIF   Oh, my God!

KARLA   What?

GRIF   We were fighting.

KARLA   We weren't fighting.

GRIF   Yes, we were!

KARLA   No we weren't!

GRIF   Yes we were!

KARLA   That was not a fight.

GRIF   Yes it was. And now it's time to kiss and make
          up. Come on. Give me a little kissy!

KARLA   Forget it!

GRIF   Kissy kissy kissy!

KARLA   Get lost!

GRIF   Pweese... a witto kissy for Gwiffy!

KARLA   Cut it out!

          SOUND: The mess hall bell rings.

GRIF   Piffle! Staff meeting.

KARLA   She's bell-happy already.

GRIF   Let's go.

KARLA   Wait, wait!

GRIF   What?

          *KARLA removes her leather bracelet and
          presents GRIF with it.*

KARLA	You wear it.
GRIF	(*reads*) It says "Let's get high."
KARLA	It has great sentimental value. I traded for it at the Ex. With Lenny the Leatherman.
GRIF	That's nice.
KARLA	Put it on.

    GRIF, embarrassed, puts it on.

KARLA	Now, give me your ring.
GRIF	Are you crazy? You can't have this ring!
KARLA	Why not?
GRIF	Because my Grandmother gave it to me when I was ten! My mother used to wear it. It's a family heirloom!
KARLA	Just for the summer.
GRIF	You'll lose it!
KARLA	I will not! It will be my most treasured item.
GRIF	But, Karla...
KARLA	Give me the ring, or I'll switch cabins with Charmagne. She farts all the time in her sleep.
GRIF	You would not.
KARLA	The ring or I'm gone!

    Pause.

GRIF	With Charmagne?

    KARLA verbally makes a flatulent noise.

Okay! Alright! For the summer. Then I want it back. You promise.

KARLA   Yeah, yeah.

GRIF   If my grandmother ever finds out I let someone else wear this ring...

          GRIF gives KARLA her ring. The mess hall bell rings again.

          That's for us. We're going to get shit already. Whoops... Piffle!

KARLA   (*raising her hand*) Your rule!

          GRIF runs out, shrieking playfully. KARLA stops to pull her knife out of the bunk.

          DANNY turns in his chair, and speaks to KARLA as if she were a child.

DANNY   What have you got in your hand, Karla?

          KARLA puts her hands behind her back and responds as a young girl.

KARLA   Nothing.

DANNY   Don't you lie to your father. Show me what you have in your hand.

KARLA   It's just a knife.

DANNY   A knife! Let me see it. Now. Or you're going to your room.

KARLA   Can I bring it with me?

DANNY   Don't be a smart ass with me, young lady. Show me the knife.

          KARLA quickly shows him, then hides it behind her again.

DANNY   Where d'you get that?

KARLA   I found it.

DANNY   You playing in my chest again in the
               basement? Huh? Give it to me.

KARLA   No, Daddy. I want it! Please?

DANNY   Karla, what is a nine-year-old girl going to do
               with a knife?

KARLA   Keep it in my pocket.

DANNY   Why?

KARLA   Because I like it! I like the way the blade
               comes out like this. See, look. It's all sharp
               and shiny. I polished it up with a face cloth.
               And then it goes back inside. Like it's hiding.

DANNY   Karla...

KARLA   I promise I'll be careful. I'll take good care of
               it. I won't do anything wrong. I just want to
               keep it in my pocket. Okay?

               *KARLA runs out. DANNY shakes his head,
               smiling.*

               *A telephone rings. GRIF's message is heard
               on the answering machine: "Hi. You've
               reached 236-3048. I'm not in right now, but if
               you leave your name and number..."*

               Grif's Apartment.
               *GRIF enters the apartment followed by
               KARLA. GRIF hurriedly dumps her bags at
               the entrance and answers the phone, turning
               off the machine.*

GRIF   Don't hang up I'm here! ... Oh, hi swee—

GRIF looks over at KARLA, then continues.

GRIF How was your day...? I'm fine...

While GRIF talks, KARLA hangs up her jacket, then brings the bags to the counter. She opens the lingerie bag and holds up and examines a sexy, feminine brassiere.

GRIF ...Oh. Darn. Well, can you still make it for seven? I can wait for you. I'll order at seven thirty. No, it's okay. See you. Bye. Yeah... (*self consciously*) Love you back.

GRIF hangs up and turns to KARLA.

KARLA (*about brassiere*) This is very nice, Grif.

GRIF Yes.

Annoyed, GRIF takes the brassiere from KARLA and brings it to the bathroom. KARLA begins unpacking the groceries. There is a bowl on the counter with a few old vegetables sticking out of it.

KARLA (*calling*) You want the tomatoes in this bowl here, or in the fridge?

GRIF I'll do that!

KARLA You should keep them in the fridge. Fresh produce spoils fast.

GRIF (*returning*) I like them in the bowl.

KARLA Nutritional loss.

GRIF Would you let me do this?

KARLA watches GRIF put away the rest of the groceries — a few vegetables, some fruit.

KARLA   You on a diet? You don't need to lose weight. Where you going to lose it from?

                GRIF is bent over.

                Your butt? There's nothing wrong with your butt. It's a perfectly acceptable butt. You still swim a lot, right?

GRIF   Yes.

KARLA   Hey, you know what I'm going to do? I'm going to make you the best Greek salad you've ever had. You got any feta?

GRIF   No, you're not.

KARLA   It's low-fat.

GRIF   I hope you don't mind reheated coffee.

                GRIF turns on the coffee machine. There is some old coffee in the carafe.

KARLA   You got an ashtray?

                GRIF hands her one.

GRIF   Would you open the window, please?

                KARLA opens the window and looks down.

KARLA   You like living on the market?

GRIF   It's convenient.

KARLA   You can watch all the hookers from here.

GRIF   I could.

                KARLA leans out the window.

KARLA   How's business today, ladies!

GRIF   Please ... Karla.

KARLA   Hey, you got any vinegar? Do a great job on this.

GRIF   Pardon?

KARLA   Vinegar. It's the best stuff for cleaning windows. All this crud from the traffic.

                KARLA searches in the cupboards.

                Where's your vinegar?

GRIF   Karla. Don't clean my windows.

KARLA   No, no really. Watch this, you'll be amazed. It'll only take a second. Where's your paper towels?

GRIF   I ran out.

KARLA   A tea towel will do.

                KARLA takes one from the counter.

GRIF   Why do you want to wash my windows?

                KARLA begins to wipe. DANNY appears on the other side of the window. KARLA stares out at him.

DANNY   I notice these things, Karla. About you. Things, that I can't figure. Your clothes: Torn. Ripped. Worn. You wear the same, damn, black tee shirt every day ... but you wash it every night. Your running shoes: Broken laces. Tied in knots. Holes wearing through the bottom ... always placed perfectly, neatly on the boot tray by the door. You never throw away a plastic container. They're all organised by size in the cupboard. You change the aluminum things under the stove burners every week. But, what gets me Karla ... is the windows. You're always washing the bloody windows. Why are you always washing the windows?

DANNY stays watching her.

KARLA   Because they're dirty.

KARLA continues washing.

KARLA   I had a janitorial job at the Met Life building for a while. That's where I learned about vinegar. This old lady? She'd been doing janitorial labour for thirty-seven years. Can you believe it? She was great. Told the dirtiest jokes. Cleanest old lady I ever met. She could clean anything. There.

GRIF   Where are you working now?

KARLA   The Delta. Salads and desserts.

GRIF   Do you like it?

KARLA   Oh, yes. It's my calling. How's psychology?

GRIF   I'm an elementary school counsellor.

KARLA   Do you like it?

GRIF   Well, it's sort of ... it's fine.

KARLA   Just fine.

GRIF   You don't get to see the happy ones.

KARLA   (*finished*) There.

GRIF   Thanks.

DANNY   You missed a spot.

DANNY exits.

KARLA   Don't mention it.

     Pause.

     Got anything to drink?

GRIF   The coffee's almost hot. You wanted to talk about your father.

KARLA   Yeah. You got anything to drink?

GRIF   You said you were straight.

KARLA   I'm in mourning. I'm entitled to the odd depressant.

GRIF   Do you feel you need a drink to talk about your father?

KARLA   Yes, Dr. Grif, I do feel that way.

GRIF   And why do you think that is?

KARLA   Sets the mood, I guess.

GRIF   What mood does it set?

KARLA   Fuck the shrink shit, Grif. I wanted to talk to you. Like we used to. I don't want all this "how does it make you feel?" crap.

     Pause.

GRIF   I have some wine.

KARLA   That'll do.

     GRIF pours her a glass.

KARLA   Aren't you going to have some?

GRIF   No.

KARLA   Come on. It'll loosen you up.

> *KARLA pours GRIF a glass.*

GRIF   I don't like to drink before dinner.

KARLA   Here you go. Cheers.

> *KARLA offers to clink glasses with GRIF.*
> *GRIF turns away.*

GRIF   Please, have a seat, Karla.

> *They move to the couch. KARLA sits casually*
> *on the arm.*

KARLA   Where's your bedroom?

GRIF   The couch folds out.

KARLA   You got a good job. Why are you living in a
bachelor?

GRIF   I'm saving.

KARLA   For what? A house?

GRIF   Yes. (*beat*) You find that amusing?

KARLA   I always figured some guy with a BMW would
provide the house.

> *Pause.*

GRIF   Your father. How did he die?

KARLA   Heart attack. What else? Smoked like a
chimney. Drank like a fish. He'd put lard on
his toast if there wasn't any butter.

GRIF   Were you with him when he had his attack?

KARLA   Yeah. We were ... arguing.

GRIF   What about?

KARLA   Something about the dragon.

GRIF   He was still...?

KARLA   Here we were, been without her for 20 years.
               Whenever he got pissed all he'd do is talk
               about her. How pretty she was, what a good
               cook she was, what a slut she was... And then
               he'd get out the wedding pictures. Can you
               believe he kept the friggin' things? And then
               he'd dribble and cry all over them. It pissed
               me off. What a waste, you know? All that
               time. So stupid!

               *DANNY enters the scene, brandishing a wet
               facecloth. He is stumbling drunk.*

DANNY   I want to know, Karla! I want to know what
               the hell happened to your nose! Eh? Why is it
               bleeding!

KARLA   Leave me alone, Danny!

DANNY   How many times I tell you not to hang out at
               the Chaud?

               *KARLA rises and crosses to **Danny's Place**,
               trying to get away from him. DANNY
               stumbles after her.*

KARLA   I wasn't at the Chaud!

DANNY   It's no place for a girl, Karla.

KARLA   I haven't been there for over a year!

DANNY   Everyone's looking to scrap there! You
               scrapping with someone?

KARLA   No!

DANNY   Girls shouldn't scrap!

KARLA   I wasn't scrapping! I wasn't at the Chaud!

DANNY   Now look at you! Scrapping at the Chaud.
               Y'into some "gang" kind-o-shit, maybe? That's
               just what I need, thank you very much, my
               daughter in one of those street scrapping gangs!

KARLA   There's no gang, Danny! I told you already I
               slipped on some ice. I bashed into the outside
               railing, okay! Right here! Outside! The stair
               railing! Scout's honour!

               DANNY reaches for her with the facecloth.

DANNY   Here...

               *KARLA tries to take it from him, but he is
               insistent on wiping her nose himself.*

KARLA   Would you just give it to me?

DANNY   Let me do it.

KARLA   No!

DANNY   Here, look at me!

KARLA   NO!

DANNY   For Christ sake, girl. When are you going to
               grow up? I'm going to clean your nose, whether
               you like it or not. Stay STILL!

KARLA   Danny, just FUCK OFF!

               *KARLA punches him hard in the chest.
               DANNY recoils, gulping and gasping,
               feigning a heart attack.*

DANNY   Karla...

KARLA   Get lost, Danny.

DANNY   You hit me, Karla.

KARLA   I told you to leave me alone!

DANNY   Pain, Karla... my heart... call the hospital.

KARLA   Aw, come on.

DANNY   Call them.

KARLA   Call them yourself.

> *KARLA gets him the phone.*

Here. Well, go ahead, Danny. Dial! Dial the phone, asshole!

> *DANNY keeps gasping, his eyes fixed on her. KARLA begins to doubt.*

Daddy? Daddy! Oh, God...

> *KARLA moves to him. He looks away from her.*

Oh God, I'm sorry! Daddy...

> *DANNY turns back to KARLA looking horrified.*

DANNY   Boo!

> *He laughs hysterically.*

KARLA   (*enraged*) You son of a bitch! Don't you ever...!

> *KARLA violently shoves him.*

> *DANNY feigns a second attack. This time, KARLA stands back from him. He staggers to the phone and attempts to dial. He gives up, beseeching with animal-like noises. Again, KARLA doubts.*

KARLA   Oh, Jesus... Jesus, Daddy... don't...

> *KARLA grabs the phone, fumbling with the number. DANNY stands and laughs again.*

KARLA   You asshole!

>*DANNY's laughter suddenly stops. His face becomes grotesquely contorted, he holds his left shoulder and falls back into his chair. KARLA moves away from him, back towards* **Grif's apartment.**

KARLA   (*moving away from him*) You're a lunatic. You hear me, Danny? You're a fucking asshole, lunatic, BASTARD!

>*DANNY struggles to form his words.*

DANNY   ...Balloons on the wall...

KARLA   (*quietly*) ...what...?

DANNY   Balloons ... on the wall...

>*DANNY dies. KARLA moves back to* **Grif's apartment.**

KARLA   He'd get so twisted. His heart all in knots.

GRIF   So, an argument about your mother brought on the attack.

KARLA   Yup.

GRIF   And what did you do? When you realised what was happening?

>*Pause.*

KARLA   Remember that CPR course we took? I was positive it was a heart attack.

GRIF   So, you performed CPR.

>*Pause.*

GRIF   Karla?

KARLA   Probably wouldn't have saved him anyway.
                 His gig was up. He was a mess.

GRIF   It's not unusual to feel responsible for the
                 death of a loved one.

KARLA   (*smirks*) "A loved one."

GRIF   Particularly if your relationship was ...
                 unstable. Afterwards, we want to have them
                 back, to solve all the problems. To say the
                 things we perhaps never said ... or do the
                 things we never did. And if you were there,
                 seeing it all ... well, it's a true shock. You were
                 in shock, Karla.

                 Sometimes when we're presented with an
                 emergency situation, even one we've even been
                 trained for, like the CPR, our senses just don't
                 work. Don't blame yourself. Your father's
                 death is not your fault.

                      KARLA pours herself another glass of wine.

KARLA   Remember that CPR course? What a grind. All
                 the practice we did on each other. You were so
                 mad at the final test, when I scored higher
                 than you.

GRIF   I wasn't mad.

KARLA   Yes, you were.

GRIF   Why would I get mad about that?

KARLA   You never liked anyone doing better than you.

GRIF   That's ridiculous.

KARLA   No it's not.

GRIF   I just like to do my best.

KARLA   You did your best. Just my best was better.

GRIF   I was disappointed in myself.

KARLA   You were really pissed off.

GRIF   Karla, I know of a very good support group. Or if you would prefer a private counsellor—

KARLA   (*laughs*) Right!

GRIF   Sitting here for a couple of minutes isn't going to help you cope with your grief.

KARLA   You always had such low self esteem.

GRIF   No, I didn't!

               KARLA smiles to herself.

               You know why you're doing this?

KARLA   What am I doing?

GRIF   You feel angry and guilty.

KARLA   Maybe.

GRIF   You want a fight.

KARLA   No I don't.

GRIF   You want someone to hurt you.

KARLA   I want a friend.

GRIF   You want a friend to hurt you. Subconsciously, it would alleviate your guilt.

KARLA   Is this what they taught you?

GRIF   Yes.

KARLA   You should ask for your money back.

GRIF   I am not going to fight with you, Karla.

KARLA   Fuck, man. I don't want to fight!

GRIF   You barge into my house...

KARLA   I didn't barge.

GRIF   Go through my groceries...

KARLA   I was helping.

GRIF   Clean my windows..

KARLA   They were dirty!

GRIF   Against my will...

> *KARLA freezes and softly emphasises and directs her words straight to GRIF.*

KARLA   I would never do anything against your will.

> *Pause.*

Would I?

> *Pause.*

GRIF   I'm not the right person to help you.

> *GRIF stands.*

I have to get ready to go.

> *GRIF takes a small swig of her wine and dumps the rest in the sink.*

KARLA   So, who is he? Another one of your big men?

Hey, you still feel the same about little dinks? What did you used to call them? "Little minnows." That was it. You used to say little men's bodies made your skin crawl. You still feel that way? About dinks?

DANNY suddenly rises.

DANNY   I think it's time we had a little talk.

GRIF   We're adults now, Karla.

DANNY crosses to GRIF's couch and leans against the back of it. He is uncomfortable with what he has to say.

DANNY   This sort of thing isn't easy to talk about. But, you see, you're uh ... well ... getting older, and ... you know what I'm trying to say...?

KARLA ignores him and continues talking to GRIF.

KARLA   You always had big guys. Jocks. Weightlifters. They all had big bones didn't they? Except that one. What was he? That student. Yeah. He studied something that he didn't need a big dink for—

DANNY   But most important, Karla...

KARLA   But, he didn't last long anyway, did he?

DANNY   Are you paying attention? This is important.

GRIF   I have to get changed.

KARLA   He just couldn't fill you up.

DANNY   Just... Well, just make sure you don't love the guy. Especially the first time.

KARLA   But then, you remember what everyone said about the size of your...

DANNY   'Cause then you're just setting yourself up to get hurt.

KARLA   ..."Peter Heater."

             DANNY turns directly to her.

DANNY   And I wouldn't want to see you get hurt by
             some useless scum.

             DANNY exits.

KARLA   Remember the night we sat up making up
             names for it? Peter heater. Love bush. Clam
             clamp.

             I'll never forget how proud you were when you
             informed all of us in Cabin Eight that you had
             been poked for the first time at boy's camp
             day. And we were all of what? Twelve,
             thirteen years old?

GRIF   I have to get ready to go, now.

KARLA   Okay. Go ahead.

GRIF   I need to have a shower.

KARLA   Fine.

GRIF   I said half an hour.

KARLA   According to my watch I still have six minutes.
             And the coffee should be ready.

             KARLA goes to get the cup of coffee.

             Go have your shower. I can answer the phone
             if it rings.

GRIF   No, that's okay.

             GRIF turns the answering machine on.

             The machine's on.

KARLA   I could take a message.

GRIF   No, thank you.

KARLA   But what if it's an emergency? Like, your grandmother having a stroke.

GRIF   My grandmother is not going to have a stroke.

KARLA   Who are you, God? You just said she wasn't well. What kind of a grand daughter are you? Who doesn't want to know if their grandmother's had a stroke or not?

GRIF   I'm going to take my shower.

KARLA   Okay. I'll let myself out when I'm finished my coffee.

GRIF   I would prefer that you leave now.

KARLA   I promise I won't steal anything. I'll leave you my address and phone number in case anything is missing when you come out.

               Oh, and thanks a lot. You were a big help. I won't feel guilty any more.

GRIF   You should think about seeing someone.

KARLA   So, I'll see you around. I'll call next time.

GRIF   I'm pretty busy these days.

KARLA   Yeah.

GRIF   Goodbye, Karla.

               KARLA smiles brightly and waves her off. GRIF goes into the bathroom. When KARLA hears the shower go on, she goes to the phone and unplugs it. Then, she takes GRIF's keys out of her raincoat, takes her own jacket and exits.

The Cabin.
GRIF bursts into the cabin wearing a bath robe. Out of the pocket she takes a cassette tape which she pops into the boom box. She takes off the robe. She wears a very tiny bikini bathing suit and practices a few dance steps. KARLA enters the cabin with an old tuxedo jacket over her arm, holding a ratty top hat and a long stick to use as a dance cane.

KARLA   TA-DAAAA!

     She places the hat on her head with a flourish.

GRIF   Oh, that's so great! I thought for sure the costume cupboard would be empty by now.

KARLA   I had to fight for them.

GRIF   Oh, "Karlo," you're my hero!

KARLA   And you my little bubble-head, are ... uh... almost naked.

     GRIF is fiddling with the straps of the bikini top.

GRIF   Can you tighten this up for me?

KARLA   Here.

     GRIF is swivelling her hips in a "bump and grind" fashion.

KARLA   Hold still, you silly bitch!

GRIF   I'm just warming up.

KARLA   I can't believe we're doing this. Minnie and Frankie did this same act for Staff Show three years ago.

GRIF   And? It was a smash hit. Everyone loves
              revivals! Anyway, this is KARLO AND GRIF,
              not Minnie and Frankie. Besides, I've got better
              goods than Minnie did, right, Karlo?

              GRIF bumps KARLA with her hip.

              Or are you a breast man?

              *GRIF slides her finger suggestively inside her
              bikini top. Embarrassed, KARLA turns away.*

              Oh, I think you are.

KARLA   I think you need more stuffing.

              GRIF whacks KARLA.

GRIF   Hey!

              *KARLA hits "play" on the boom box. It plays
              Chris De Burg's "Patricia The Stripper."*

              *Using the song, they rehearse their ridiculous
              "Karlo and Grif" act — The Backwards
              Strip-Tease. KARLA plays the part of the
              narrator — and sings the first part of the song
              to the audience, indicating to GRIF as
              "Patricia" — who poses and 'vogues' coyly to
              the side.
              With the chorus "...and with a swing of her
              hips..." GRIF begins to dress over her bikini
              in oversized rain pants, coat, gumboots and
              sou'wester. KARLA hands her the clothes
              and helps her with the boots. It should be
              playfully choreographed fun.
              When GRIF finishes dressing with some sort
              of flourish to indicate the end of the act,
              KARLA drops the "Karlo" persona and
              attempts to turn the music off. GRIF, instead,
              continues to dance in a sexually overt fashion
              and rubs herself against KARLA, taking off
              KARLA's hat and coat, giggling, cavorting,*

> *etc., making KARLA terribly embarrassed and uncomfortable.*

KARLA   Grif. What are you... Come on. Stop it!

> *She becomes angry and forcefully pushes GRIF away.*

Cut it out!

GRIF   What?

> *KARLA exits.*

Karla! I'm just... I'm just...!

> *SOUND: Slamming house door.*

> **Danny's Place**
> *DANNY is looking at the photo album. KARLA enters with her gear as if she has just returned from camp.*

DANNY   (*surprised*) Hey! Hey! When the hell did you get back?

KARLA   Just now.

DANNY   I didn't know when to expect you. How'd you get here?

KARLA   I took the bus.

DANNY   With all your stuff? Why didn't you call me? I would have come and got you.

> *Pause.*

Well, come here and hug your old man. Come here, come here, I'm not going to bite you.

> *KARLA allows herself to be hugged.*

DANNY   Oh, my baby girl! Look at you! All tanned and
         beautiful! You look so ... healthy! How was
         your summer, eh? Hey, uh... How's your arm?
         Hm? All right?

KARLA   Yeah, fine.

DANNY   Stupid accident. I had a hell of a summer
         thinking about you, Karla. But you know
         what? It's going to change. I'm going to change.
         All this fighting between you and me. That's
         it. It's through. No more. I can't stand it when
         you're not here for so long. No more arguments,
         no more accidents. Okay?

KARLA   I'm moving out, Dad.

DANNY   Come on. Don't start that.

KARLA   I'm going to start looking for a place tomorrow.

DANNY   Come on, Karla. You just got in.

KARLA   I thought you'd want to know.

DANNY   Hey. You moving in with a guy? What guy is
         this?

KARLA   I should get a place closer to Algonquin maybe.

DANNY   What for?

KARLA   It takes forty-five minutes to get there by bus,
         that's what for.

DANNY   What? What? You're going to college? What
         the hell is this? A miracle?

KARLA   I worked it out over the summer. I'm going to
         take Hotel Management.

DANNY   Hey! That's great! Hotel Management, eh?
         You know, Joyce used to work the night desk
         at—

KARLA   Dad.

DANNY   Yeah. Well. That's good, Karla. I'm proud of you, Baby. But why move out? I could help you with a down payment for a car if that's the problem.

KARLA   No, no. Thanks, Dad.

DANNY   So who's this guy you're moving in with? You meet him over the summer?

KARLA   Nobody! I didn't say that — you did!

DANNY   Well, let's not talk about this now, okay?

            Pause.

            Hey, how about we go out for dinner? Eh? Would you like that?

            We'll get dressed. I could wear that jacket you got me last Christmas. Never seen me in that jacket. Looks real nice. Yeah. (*sniffs*) You'd better have a shower first. (*laughs*)

            Where would you like to go? Huh? The Keg? Eh? Grab a steak? I bet you haven't been eating too much steak this summer, eh? What do you say? Salad bar. Litre of red. You and me. Okay, Karla? Let's go.

KARLA   Danny, I... I'm really tired.

DANNY   You still mad at me, Karla? Is that it? I told you already. I'm really sorry. It's going to stop. I'm slowing down on the drinking. It's true. Come here. Let me hold you.

            DANNY holds her and rocks her tenderly. KARLA holds back tears.

DANNY   You're my baby. You always will be. I want
               you with me, sweetie. We need each other, you
               know? I love you, honey.

               Let me buy you a car.

KARLA   Dad, no. That's not it.

DANNY   Well, what then? What is it? Hey, are you
               crying? Why are you crying like this?

KARLA   I'm not crying. I'm going to bed.

               KARLA exits.

DANNY   But you haven't eaten yet! What's your
               problem?

               The Cabin.
               *GRIF enters the dark cabin sounding
               extremely worn out, and looking rather
               dishevelled.*

GRIF   I'm back...

DANNY   Eh, Karla?

GRIF   Karla?

DANNY   You not hungry?

GRIF   I can't see!

DANNY   Don't you want to talk to me?

GRIF   Turn on your light!

DANNY   Eh?

               GRIF is feeling the bottom bunk for KARLA.

GRIF   Karla? Hey. Where are you when I need you?
               Where's my welcome? Where's my backrub?

*KARLA enters, shining her flashlight in
GRIF's eyes.*

KARLA   You made it.

GRIF   (*whining*) Yeah. Where were you?

KARLA   Putting out a grease fire. I'm a hero.

GRIF   Bull.

KARLA   Staff lounge.

GRIF   Why?

KARLA   What do you mean?

GRIF   I wanted you here.

KARLA   So, I'm here.

GRIF   Were you rubbing someone else's back?

KARLA   You want one?

GRIF   Were you?

KARLA   Would it matter if I was?

GRIF   Maybe.

KARLA   I was teaching Fran how to roll Drum tobacco
               in strawberry rolling papers. You know, you can
               chew those papers if you get really bored.

GRIF   Gross.

KARLA   Roll over. So how was it?

               GRIF moans.

               Great thunderstorm, eh?

GRIF   Spectacular.

KARLA   How were the lakes?

GRIF   Enormous.

KARLA   One little overnight should be a cinch for
            "senior waterfront".

GRIF   Rub, please.

            KARLA straddles GRIF's back and digs in.
            GRIF enjoys the rub loudly.

KARLA   So, what's the scoop? How did it go? Any
            jumpers?

GRIF   No Kamikaze canoers.

KARLA   Tribal wars?

GRIF   No fights.

KARLA   Leaking tents?

GRIF   Uh-uh.

KARLA   Well, why are you so beat, then?

GRIF   You don't want to know.

KARLA   Yes, I do.

GRIF   No, you don't.

KARLA   (*digging hard*) Yes... I... do!

GRIF   Ow! Ow! Okay, okay!

            Wigapee Boy's Camp was doing their
            overnight on the other side of the island.

KARLA   So, why couldn't you find another island?

GRIF	Are you crazy? We've been up here for seven weeks, Karla. All girls, remember? Besides, we were there first. And you should have seen their trip leader.
KARLA	Uh huh.
GRIF	Adonis in person.
KARLA	Really.
GRIF	Six foot one, pure blond, and stomach muscles ... you know those ones ... the little squares they get? And biceps that made me howl.
KARLA	You saw all this in the rain?
GRIF	We went for a swim.
KARLA	A swim?
GRIF	A dip.
KARLA	In a thunder storm?
GRIF	OW! OW! Jesus!
KARLA	What?
GRIF	That really hurt.

> *KARLA lifts up GRIF's shirt and shines the flashlight on her back.*

KARLA	Holy shit! What happened?
GRIF	What?
KARLA	You should see this!
GRIF	I can't! Tell me!
KARLA	Shit. Your back is a mess.

GRIF   What, Karla, would you tell me what it is?

KARLA   It's all scratched and there's a big bruise right here ...

GRIF   Ow!

KARLA   What happened?

GRIF giggles.

What?

GRIF   I'll bet his knees are like raw meat.

Pause.

KARLA   You are such a slut!

GRIF   Under a blue spruce.

KARLA   You sure it wasn't a balsam?

GRIF   It was amazing, Karla. I have never done it outside in a thunderstorm, before.

KARLA   Yes, it is amazing that you'd never done it outside in a thunderstorm, before. Couldn't you just carve your initials in a tree for a change?

GRIF   If you're not going to rub you can get off my back.

KARLA resumes rubbing.

Just watch that bruise. Oh, Karla. It was so perfect. When the thunder rolled I could scream my heart out. God, did I scream.

KARLA   That's nice.

GRIF   I am so sore.

KARLA   I really feel for you.

GRIF   I am so tired.

KARLA   Go to sleep and shut up.

GRIF   Okay.

              KARLA keeps rubbing as GRIF falls asleep.
              She gently strokes GRIF's hair and longingly,
              preciously holds a lock of it. She then rises
              and tiptoes out of the cabin. As she gets to the
              door, DANNY calls out. She turns to face
              him, but he is calling to KARLA down the
              hallway.

              Danny's Place.

DANNY   So, Karla! About this guy. What is he? A life
              guard? Or ... a canoeing instructor? Don't tell
              me... You were sneaking out at night and
              meeting up with the lads from the boys' camp,
              weren't ya? (*chuckles*) Weren't ya? I wasn't
              born yesterday you know.

              So, when do I get to meet him? Eh? When do I
              get to do the "heavy father stuff"? Ha ha.
              Scare the shit out of him. Come on, Karla.
              Bring him home. I promise I won't bite.

              KARLA exits the cabin, shaking her head.

              Aw, come on!

              Grif's Apartment.
              GRIF, with a towel wrapped around her hair,
              pokes her head out of the bathroom, checking
              to see that KARLA is gone. She goes to the
              door to ensure it is locked. As she turns to go
              back to the bathroom, she hears keys fumbling
              clumsily in the door. A moment of
              recognition. She smiles.

GRIF   (*cheerily*) Hey, Darlin'! What are you doing
              here? I thought we were going to meet at the
              DeLuxe? (beat) You're going to snap the key if

you keep forcing it like that! You turn the key to the left, the knob to the right and you push it in before you pull it out!

The door is successfully unlocked.

See?

She realises she is wearing only her lingerie.

Oh, wait a second! I don't want you to see my surprise, yet!

She runs back into the bathroom.

Okay!

KARLA steps in the door with a small bag and a bottle of wine. She hangs up her jacket and brings the items to the counter.

GRIF   (*loudly*) I'm just going to finish drying my hair...

A blow-dryer is heard.

I'm glad, you're here. I'd rather eat in tonight, anyway, wouldn't you? I had a weird day. Hey, I could make us a salad. Greek. Would you like that? Except I don't have any feta. But, I could pop down to Kardish's and get some. And we could just watch television or something. I sure could use one of your rubs. Oh, yeah.

The blow-dryer stops.

And then I'll rub yours...

GRIF pokes her head out of the bathroom. KARLA smiles and holds up the bag.

KARLA   I already got the feta.

GRIF is shocked.

KARLA   I checked. You were out. Here's your keys. I'll just leave them here.

     KARLA starts getting the things out to make a salad.

KARLA   So, what's the surprise?

GRIF   What do you think you're doing?

KARLA   Oh, and I bought some more wine. You want a glass while you're waiting?

GRIF   No! Look. You can't... Karla, you ... Okay. You obviously have... You have a problem. I recognise that. But, this is not... This is no way... okay ... alright... Look...

KARLA   Just say what you mean, Grif.

GRIF   Let's you and me make a real appointment, and we'll work this out in a mature fashion.

KARLA   An appointment?

     KARLA looks in the fridge.

GRIF   Okay, Karla. You want an apology? Is that it?

KARLA   I did see a lemon in here, didn't I?

GRIF   Alright. Karla, I'm sorry. I acted immaturely. And irresponsibly.

     KARLA finds a lemon.

KARLA   Aha! You squeeze it on the romaine.

GRIF   It was unfair. I'll admit it. Unfair. But, I was confused. Confused and immature. It should never have happened.

KARLA   Keeps it crisp and gives it a nice kick.

GRIF   Did you hear me?

KARLA   You really are tense.

GRIF   It was over three years ago!

KARLA   Have a seat. I'll do your neck.

GRIF   I have to go in five minutes. And would you
           stop tearing my lettuce?

KARLA   Where's your colander?

           *GRIF goes to the kitchen and starts putting
           things away.*

GRIF   I don't want you to make me a salad.

KARLA   Don't worry. I'm a professional.

GRIF   You are not making me a salad!

KARLA   You just said you wanted a salad!

GRIF   I am meeting someone for dinner! I will order a
           salad at the restaurant!

KARLA   So, this "someone" has keys to your
           apartment? Must be a pretty important
           someone. Damn, do you have black olives?

GRIF   This is unbelievable.

KARLA   Tell me, do you often just sit at home and
           watch T.V.? That's quite a switch from the old
           party-girl, isn't it?

           Party, party, party. Guys, guys, guys. You
           always had to be the centre. The more guys
           dripping off you the better. No conscience at
           all for all those weasels who fell for every
           sway of your ass, every jiggle of your tits.

You'd wear your skimpiest bikini to Boy's Camp Day. Christ, even the eight-year-old boys were wagging their tails after you.

So, what happened to you, anyway? What's happened to change you into a "homebody". Someone who's happy with just one person. Watching T.V. Eating salad. You are happy, aren't you? You sure sounded happy when I walked in.

That is so weird. I never expected it, boy.

Ah! Good taste in olive oil.

GRIF   Get out of my house.

                KARLA pulls out her pocket knife and holds it above her head.

KARLA   The Sabre! (*diabolically*) Ha ha ha ha ha!

                KARLA viciously slices a tomato with it.

                Take that! And that!

GRIF   Stop it!

KARLA   (*stops*) Oh. Do you prefer it in wedges?

GRIF   You have to leave. I'M GOING OUT!

KARLA   Oh. Right. Your date called. He got held up. Won't be able to make it after all.

                GRIF looks at KARLA carefully.

                While you were in the shower?

                The phone rang.

                I couldn't help myself.

                She slaps her own hand.

KARLA   Bad, Karla, bad.

        Pause.

        So. Looks like you're free for dinner.

        But uh,

        You might want to put on something a little more ... comfortable.

        End of Act One.

Act Two

The Apartment.
KARLA is alone in the kitchen, assembling the salad. DANNY leans over the counter.

DANNY   What are you doing, Karla?

KARLA   Making a salad.

DANNY   No, no. What are you doing, Karla?

KARLA does not look at him.

KARLA   Making ... a ... salad.

DANNY   What are you doing to yourself, Karla?

KARLA turns to look at him.

The Cabin.
GRIF exuberantly enters the cabin with a handful of letters.

GRIF   Mail man!

KARLA and DANNY remain locked in eye contact.

DANNY   I miss ya, honey.

GRIF   I said, the mail came!

KARLA crosses into the cabin.

KARLA   Anything for me?

GRIF   Oh, now, let's see. Janet Griffiths. Miss Janet
                Griffiths. Ms. Jan Griffiths. Oh, wait a
                minute... Something illegible written by a
                "Victor Staletti? Stiletto? ... I can't...

KARLA   STILT!

GRIF   Victor Stillecki?

KARLA   Just Vic Stilt.

GRIF   And no return address. What's he in, grade
                two?

KARLA   Give me the letter.

GRIF   Truth or Dare... Who's Vic Stilt?

KARLA   A buddy.

GRIF   Just a buddy?

KARLA   Yeah, just a buddy.

GRIF   Give me the scoop, or it gets the torch.

KARLA   Just give it to me!

                GRIF hands her the letter.

GRIF   Woo. He must be some important buddy, this
                "Stilt" person. What is he, tall or something?

                *KARLA lifts the letter up to the light and
                examines it. Then she carefully pulls the stamp
                off the letter.*

                Have you become a philatelist, Karla? I find
                this quite remarkable. I mean who would
                have ever thought...

                *KARLA looks closely at the underside of the
                stamp.*

KARLA   YES! Way to go, Victor! My ticket to dream land!

> *KARLA drops the envelope. GRIF picks it up and opens it. It is empty.*

GRIF   Didn't he learn that the letter goes *in* the envelope?

KARLA   This is a gift of love. No words are necessary.

GRIF   What is it?

> *KARLA is delicately removing the acid from the back of the stamp.*

KARLA   It's a hit of windowpane.

GRIF   What?

KARLA   Lysergic Acid Diethylemide.

GRIF   No. No way. You're not going to take acid up here.

KARLA   Tomorrow's my day off, remember?

GRIF   You were going off that stuff. You promised. Last year. No more acid.

KARLA   And you promised no more one-nighters. You broke it first. Ha ha!

GRIF   Give it to me.

KARLA   Yeah, right.

GRIF   Come on, Karla.

KARLA   Hey... you want half? Come on, do half with me.

GRIF   No way.

KARLA   A quarter. I'll give you a quarter. Just a weenie
             trip. It'd be fun!

GRIF   Forget it!

             GRIF pushes KARLA's hand away.

KARLA   Hey! Oh, shit! I dropped it!

             *KARLA frantically searches for the hit on her
             hands and knees. While KARLA searches,
             GRIF sees it and manages to pick it up and
             hide it.*

             If I lose it, I'll kill you. Two months. Two
             months, Grif, I haven't had a hit!

GRIF   Look at you.

KARLA   Get down and help me find it!

GRIF   You're pathetic.

KARLA   This is my night out! It doesn't come and pick
             me up in a BMW! It comes on a little
             rectangular tab. And I want it. NOW! So, help
             me find it!

             *DANNY approaches KARLA. She ignores
             him, directing her comments to GRIF.*

DANNY   What are you doing to yourself, Karla?

GRIF   Are you addicted, Karla? I could help you if
             you're addicted.

DANNY   Look me in the eyes.

KARLA   No, I'm not addicted. You are so goddamned
             ignorant!

GRIF   I'm not ignorant.

DANNY   What do you think, I'm stupid?!

KARLA   You're stupid! You don't know anything about
            it.

DANNY   You want to ruin your life on this shit!

KARLA   Shit! I'm never going to find it in these cracks.
            I'm going to kill you!

GRIF   You swore.

DANNY   I won't have it in my house!

KARLA   I don't give a flying fuck about your shitty
            rules.

GRIF   Karla, don't you enjoy my company?

KARLA   Not at the moment.

DANNY   Drinking I can understand. But this—

GRIF   We could do something else for your night off.

KARLA   I don't want to play cocksucking scrabble!

GRIF   I can't believe you're acting like this.

DANNY   You need some help or something?

KARLA   LIKE WHAT!

GRIF   Like that. I was only trying to help you.

DANNY   I can't stand seeing you like this, Karla.

KARLA   Get down on your knees and look, then.

            GRIF kneels down beside KARLA.

GRIF   Karla, I really care about you, you know. As
            strange a person as you are, I worry about your
            well-being.

DANNY   I'm your father. I worry.

KARLA	Shut up and look.
GRIF	Remember last summer when I thought I was pregnant, and you snuck into town to buy a pregnancy test for me?
KARLA	No.
GRIF	Yes, you do. Remember, when Boss Lady took that group for the day trip, and you stole her keys, and drove the van into town—
KARLA	Are you looking?
GRIF	I owed you. I lost that hit, because I care about you.
DANNY	Look, I know I don't always show it too well.
KARLA	You care about me.
GRIF	You're a good person, Karla.
DANNY	You're still my little girl in there.
KARLA	Fuck off.
GRIF	This stuff takes that away.
KARLA	(*despairing*) Oh, God, it must have slipped through the boards.
GRIF	Are you crying, Karla?
DANNY	What's the matter?
KARLA	No, I'm not crying.
DANNY	Why are you looking at me like that?
GRIF	Yes you are.
KARLA	I'm not!

DANNY   Stop it Karla. It's just me.

GRIF   Don't be mad.

DANNY   Hey! Look! This is ME!

KARLA   You've ruined my night off!

GRIF   No, no! We'll have fun. We could have a pow
           wow on the beach.

DANNY   It's the drugs, Karla! Just the drugs making you
           think that!

KARLA   Fuck that! I want to get fried!

DANNY   I wouldn't hurt you!

GRIF   You don't like me.

DANNY   Listen to me! You straighten out! Now!

KARLA   SHUT UP!

                    DANNY retreats.   Pause.

GRIF   Want me to rub your back?

KARLA   No.

GRIF   Brush your hair?

KARLA   No.

GRIF   We could pierce our ears.

KARLA   I'm going to pierce your tit if you don't leave
           me alone.

GRIF   All right, fine. You're hopeless. (*beat*) I know
           where it is.

KARLA   What? Where!

GRIF   Say you're sorry.

KARLA   Eat shit. Where is it!

GRIF   Hot and cold.

KARLA   Just tell me you stupid bitch.

GRIF   You're cold, very cold.

KARLA   Come on!

GRIF   Still cold.

              *KARLA begins moving slowly around the
              room.*

KARLA   I'll get you for this.

GRIF   Warm. Cold. Warmer. Warmer. Cold. Freezing
              Hot... HOT... BOILING!

              *KARLA finds the hit of acid wherever GRIF
              has hidden it.*

KARLA   Oh, God!

              She places the hit under her tongue.

GRIF   You're doing it now?

KARLA   There's no time like the present.

GRIF   How can somebody who's not addicted be so
              desperate for a stupid hit of door pane?

              KARLA bursts out laughing.

              What are you laughing at?

KARLA   (*hysterically*) "Door pane!"

GRIF   Well, excuse me.

KARLA	"Door pane!"
GRIF	I'm going to staff lounge.
KARLA	I'm going, too.
GRIF	Not on acid, you're not.
KARLA	You can't leave me here.
GRIF	Why not?
KARLA	Because.
GRIF	Because why?
KARLA	Because I always do it with someone.
GRIF	Too bad. You should have thought about that before you took it.

> *GRIF turns to leave. KARLA grabs her arm.*

GRIF	Ow!
KARLA	Please stay.
GRIF	Would you let go of my arm?
KARLA	Stay with me.
GRIF	You want a babysitter, Karla? You afraid of a bad trip? Like last year, when you were sure your father was in the closet?
KARLA	That was an accident.
GRIF	You wanna do that stuff, you do it without me.
KARLA	Come on, Grif. I've covered your ass every time you trip over to the boys camp. One night. That's all.

GRIF   It's not my day off tomorrow. I'm not staying up all night.

KARLA   If you're here... Just be here. I won't bug you. I promise. Please?

                          Pause.

GRIF   Why do I always get sucked in?

KARLA   Because you're a nice person.

                          KARLA smiles at her.

GRIF   Wanna play a game?

KARLA   Sure.

GRIF   I spy with my little eye, something that is red.

                          Danny's Place.
                          DANNY brings a suit bag to his chair. A large red Christmas bow on the bag catches KARLA's eye. She stands still, watching DANNY, talking to GRIF.

GRIF   (*waiting*) Karla?

                          KARLA takes a deep, satisfied breath and addresses GRIF.

KARLA   There is nothing like the feeling of the impending wave.

GRIF   What?

KARLA   Oh, shit. I didn't eat. I should eat something. There's leftover chicken in the breezeway fridge.

GRIF   You want me to get it, right?

KARLA   Be quick.

GRIF   You owe me.

                GRIF exits.
                KARLA watches DANNY as he unzips the
                bag and pulls out the casual jacket KARLA
                has given to him for Christmas.
                He puts it on. He is very proud and a little
                embarrassed as he displays it to her. KARLA
                is very happy. DANNY then pours two
                glasses of wine, and holds one out to KARLA,
                who crosses to take it. They clink glasses.
                DANNY gives her a small kiss, then settles
                into his chair and turns on the television.

                The Apartment.
                GRIF is seated on the couch, picking at the
                salad that KARLA has made. KARLA stands
                behind GRIF, sipping her wine and watching
                her.

KARLA   You know what this reminds me of? Monk's
                dinner. Remember Monk's dinner at camp? The
                night no talking was allowed at the table?
                And the table that lasted the longest was
                given double Rice Krispy Squares for night
                snack?

                Except you're the only monk.

                More wine?

GRIF   No.

KARLA   Oh, well. More for me. So. How was the
                salad?

GRIF   Good.

KARLA   That was better than good, Grif. That was
                excellent.

                GRIF rises to take her dishes to the counter.

KARLA   No, no. Sit down. Sit down. Tonight, I am at your service.

                 (*a little threateningly*) SIT!

                 > GRIF sits. KARLA takes the dishes to the counter, then comes back and stands behind GRIF and puts her hands on GRIF's shoulders.

KARLA   You still seem pretty tense. I think you should let me rub your neck. Then I'll do the dishes. Then I'll go.

GRIF   No.

KARLA   "No." to rub your neck? Or "No." to do the dishes.

GRIF   Why don't you go home?

KARLA   Because I'm lonely at home. No Mamma, no Poppa. Hey, I know. You wanted to watch TV. What do you like? Eh?

                 > KARLA takes the remote and turns on the television, surfing channels.

GRIF   I don't really...

KARLA   You said you were just going to stay in. You like this? I do. We'll just watch the pictures. So we can talk.

                 > KARLA begins to massage GRIF's shoulders.

GRIF   Karla, my neck is fine, really.

KARLA   (*squeezing*) You call this fine? You call this...

GRIF   Ow!

KARLA   See? Don't fight it, Grif. Don't fight it. When you've got a sore spot, you gotta take care of it.

Smooth it out. Work it over. Until the pain is gone. Right?

Pause.

KARLA   You know, you were important to me, Grif. I thought I was important to you. Part of your show. "Grif's Wacky Sidekick." I made you more interesting. You wanted it that way. You needed it. I was happy to be it. Really happy, Grif. Really, really happy.

Pause.

So. I was thinking maybe we could just pick it up. Like before. I mean, I don't exactly remember what happened, do you?

GRIF   My life is really full right now, Karla.

KARLA   I'm not asking you to marry me, Grif. I just want to be friends again.

GRIF   (*carefully*) I feel we've moved in different directions.

KARLA   We were always different, Grif. That's what you liked!

So, forgive and forget?

GRIF   I don't want to continue this! I don't appreciate the way you've manipulated this situation, and I feel it would be best for you to go now.

KARLA   Oh, come on now, Grif! Don't get all tense here, or we'll have to start all over.

Just be quiet. Don't say anything.

Danny's Place.
From his chair, DANNY clears his throat and directs his remote control to GRIF's

> *television, turning it off. KARLA reacts to*
> *him from her position in apartment.*

KARLA   Hey, I was watching that!

DANNY   It's a re-run.

KARLA   Well, what else is on?

DANNY   Karla, I want to talk to you for a minute.

KARLA   What.

DANNY   It's Friday night.

KARLA   So?

DANNY   So, why aren't you out? With your friends? At the Chaud?

KARLA   You don't like my friends.

DANNY   That never stopped you before.

KARLA   I don't feel like it.

DANNY   Why not?

KARLA   I just don't. Would you turn the TV back on?

DANNY   Look, Karla, I know we sometimes don't talk too good to each other, but you gotta let me in here. You haven't gone out for weeks. Now, why is that?

> *KARLA crosses to Danny's Place.*

KARLA   Look, Danny... you were right. Okay? I'm sick of those people. I'm sick of the Chaud. I go to school all week. I'm tired.

DANNY   Well, what about this "Grif" person?

> *Pause.*

KARLA   What about her?

DANNY   Why don't you go out with her somewhere?

KARLA   She's at University. She's busy.

DANNY   You try to get in touch with her?

KARLA   Once or twice.

             Pause.

DANNY   Why are you lying to me, Karla?

KARLA   What? I'm not—

DANNY   Don't bullshit me. What's going on?

KARLA   What's going on where?

DANNY   With this Grif person?

KARLA   Nothing.

DANNY   You're lying to me.

KARLA   About what?

DANNY   You haven't called her once or twice. You been calling her everyday. For weeks. Sometimes two or three times!

KARLA   Who told you this?

DANNY   I got a call today. From an old lady. A Mrs. Griffiths. Said you'd been harassing her granddaughter. Saying some ugly things about her. Is this true? You harassing her?

KARLA   It's none of your business.

DANNY   It sure as hell is my business. When I get called from someone's Grandmother, it's my business. Why are you harassing her?

KARLA	I just want to talk to her.
DANNY	Two or three times a day?
KARLA	She won't come to the phone.
DANNY	Why not?
KARLA	I guess she doesn't want to talk to me.
DANNY	Why not?
KARLA	Just drop it, Danny. Okay?
DANNY	No. You tell me. You tell me why she doesn't want to talk to you.
KARLA	Because she doesn't like me, I guess!
DANNY	Why not?
KARLA	We had a fight at camp!
DANNY	So, why don't you drop it, then! Someone doesn't like you, then fuck 'em! You can't have the whole world, Karla!
KARLA	I'm not asking for the whole world!
DANNY	So, what's so special about this Grif person! That you should be harassing her grandmother! Eh? Karla! Talk to me!
KARLA	No.
DANNY	You can tell me. I'm your father for God's sake. I'm sick of seeing you sitting here every Friday night. What's your problem? Boys?
KARLA	There's no fucking problem. Just keep your stupid face out of it, Okay, Dan!
DANNY	Don't you use that tone of voice with me.

KARLA   You don't like my tone of voice, I'll just leave, okay?

> *KARLA moves to exit. DANNY grabs her arm.*

DANNY   Don't you walk out on me here, Karla.

KARLA   (*menacing*) Let go of my fucking arm!

DANNY   What is it about this Grif person!

> *KARLA pushes him.*

KARLA   Grif! GRIF! It's her name! She's a girl! Not a 'Grif person', you stupid ass!

DANNY   Why you doing this, Karla? Eh? ANSWER ME! WHY!

KARLA   Because I love her!

> *Pause.*

DANNY   Pardon me?

KARLA   Listen real carefully here, Danny. 'Cause I'm not telling you again. I love Grif.

DANNY   Like a friend.

KARLA   Like a lover.

> *Pause.*

DANNY   You're in love with a girl, Karla?
You're a goddamned lesbian?
A DYKE?
Explain this to me Karla! How the hell does my daughter end up being a queer?

Do they even call girls "queers"?

KARLA   IT'S NOT LIKE THAT! It's not girls. It's HER!

DANNY   Her! HER! Well SHE'S A GIRL. And you're a girl. So that makes you a lesbian, right?

KARLA   You just can't shut up and leave me alone, can you, Danny? You can never keep out of it. So now you know. I love her. And she doesn't love me. Is that so hard to understand? You should know about this, Danny!

DANNY   So, this is what goes on in those girls camps, eh? I sent you all those summers to an all-girls camp thinking I was protecting you from being jumped by little boys!

KARLA   It's got nothing to do with the camp, Dan.

DANNY   I should have got married again. That's what you needed wasn't it?

KARLA   No!

DANNY   A woman in the house. A goddamned mother, instead of me!

KARLA   NO!

DANNY   And now, you're turning to this Grif bitch.

KARLA   JUST GRIF!

DANNY   *(crying)* Oh, Jesus. Oh, JESUS!

KARLA   Don't cry, Danny. Please. I can't stand it when you do that!

DANNY   You're gonna end up just like your mother.

        Pause.

KARLA   Don't you ever, ever say that again.

DANNY   Hanging around bars. Picking up strange men. Oh, God ... strange WOMEN!

KARLA   For Christ sake, Danny!

DANNY   And then one day... poof! Gone!

KARLA   I'm not going to leave you like that.

DANNY   She'd slime in after she'd been out all night.

KARLA   I'm not like her!

DANNY   With anyone. Anyone but me. And I'd make
            her a goddamned cup of coffee. You believe
            that, Karla?

            The Apartment.
            *Dim lighting. KARLA stays in Danny's
            place.*
            *GRIF is curled up with a pillow on the
            apartment couch, as if she were on the bottom
            bunk, speaking up to KARLA.*

GRIF   Karla? Karla are you awake?

DANNY   She'd be out prancing around with some other
            man all night, and I'd make her coffee.

GRIF   I had a bad dream.

DANNY   One morning, she comes in. Gets a suitcase, says
            she's leaving.

GRIF   About the air plane.

DANNY   That was it.

GRIF   My mother. On the air plane. She was looking
            down at me. And her teeth were falling out...

DANNY   She just left.

GRIF   I saw her teeth, Karla. Falling from the sky.

DANNY   But, did I leave you, Karla?

GRIF   Can I sleep with you?

DANNY   Eh?

GRIF   Please?

DANNY   Did I leave you?

KARLA   No.

GRIF   I'm scared.

            Lights out on GRIF.

DANNY   You were five years old. I fought off the
            goddamn Children's Aid. They wanted you in
            a foster home. They said it would be easier for
            me to let someone else look after you.

            DANNY grabs KARLA by the shoulders.

            But, did I let them take you away? Did I let
            them!

KARLA   NO!

            DANNY holds KARLA painfully close.

DANNY   You're goddamn right I didn't let them take
            you.
            I can do it!, I said. I can look after my own
            daughter! Let me look after her! I have a job!
            I have a brain! Leave us alone! Get out of my
            house!

KARLA   Danny... please.

DANNY   I was the one, Karla. I was the one who raised
            you. Me. No one else.

            I braided your hair. I washed your face. I gave
            you your medicine. I went to the parent-teacher
            meetings. I took you shopping for clothes.
            Didn't I?

DANNY   I made sure you had enough. You had what
               you needed. Didn't you? You got what you
               wanted. Didn't you? Did you eat? Did you
               have Christmas presents? Did you have
               birthday cake?

               DID YOU HAVE FUCKING SUMMER CAMP!

KARLA   YES!

DANNY   AND FOR WHAT? FOR WHAT?

                    KARLA tries to hug DANNY.

KARLA   ... Daddy...

                    DANNY shakes her off.

DANNY   What are we doing here, Karla.

               What are we doing here?

                    The Cabin.
                    It is the Last Night of Camp.
                    GRIF takes the bottle of wine from the
                    apartment, and staggers into the cabin,
                    singing into the bottle as a microphone. She is
                    really drunk.

GRIF   "And nowwwww, the end is neeeaaarrr, and so
               I face the final cuuurrtainnn...

                    KARLA regards GRIF, somewhat amused.

               La laaaa, la la la laaaa, la la la laaa....

                    KARLA crosses to her and tries to take the
                    bottle.

KARLA   Give me that.

                    GRIF holds the bottle above her head.

GRIF   Fuck you, Babboo!

KARLA   Come on, we gotta sign the boards. You won't feel like doing it tomorrow.

> *KARLA climbs up the bunk with a big magic marker. GRIF stands, wobbling, looking around the cabin.*

GRIF   Tomorrow.
Tomorrow, we leave.
We're out of here.
Not a trace. Not a speck.
Except for our names.
Names painted on the walls. Names without faces.
In years to come, people will come in here and read our names.

> *She collapses on the bottom bunk.*

What the hell does it all mean, eh, Karla? I mean, who's gonna give a shit ten years from now who "Karla and Grif" were. EH? I mean...

> *She reads a signature on the wall.*

...who the fuck is "Charlotte and Binny?"

KARLA   You're breaking the swearing rule.

GRIF   Tonight, we're allowed to break the rules.

KARLA   Are you going to sign?

GRIF   I bet these walls have seen a lot of things. A lot of secrets. Secret walls.

KARLA   You want me to do it?

GRIF   Shhhh! Walls with secrets.

KARLA   Fine, I'll do it. You never could hold your liquor.

GRIF   Oh, yeah? Oh, yeah. My liquor.

> *GRIF takes another swig from her bottle.*
> *KARLA comes back down.*

KARLA   There. "Karla and Grif. I988." Look.

> *GRIF hollers, drunkenly.*

GRIF   WooooOOOOOO! WooooOOOOOOO!

KARLA   Hey, give me that. I don't want to clean up
your puke again this year.

> *KARLA takes the bottle.*

GRIF   Like last year.

KARLA   I never figured out how it got on the ceiling.

> *They laugh.*

Give me your foot.

> *KARLA takes GRIF's shoes off.*

GRIF   Oh, Karla. You take such good care of me.

KARLA   Yes I do.

GRIF   You care about me, don't you?

KARLA   Yes, I do.

GRIF   You're my best friend, aren't you? Are you my
best friend?

KARLA   I'm your best friend.

GRIF   (*whining*) I hate the end of camp. Now I have
to go back to school. Waaaa!

KARLA   And you'll do great, as always.

GRIF   And you're going to college.

KARLA	Yeah, yeah.
GRIF	You promise now?
KARLA	I promise.
GRIF	No screwing up.
KARLA	I'll be a picture of scholarity.
GRIF	And we're coming back again next year, right, Karla?
KARLA	Sure.
GRIF	You promise.
KARLA	Scout's honour.
GRIF	Hey, I know...

GRIF pulls her sleeping bag down to the floor.

... let's have a sleep-over!

KARLA	What about "Mr. T."?
GRIF	Fuck "Mr. T."

GRIF grabs her hairbrush.

I'm armed!

GRIF pats the floor beside her.

Come on!

KARLA carefully pulls her bag down beside GRIF's.

GRIF	Brush my hair?
KARLA	What for?

GRIF   Because it feels good. And I won't have you to
          do it for me for a whole year.

KARLA   Nine and a half months.

GRIF   Pleeease?

          *KARLA kneels behind GRIF, brushing her
          hair.*

          Mmmm. I love that.

          Pause.

          Have you ever wondered why we don't see
          each other between summers?

          Pause.

KARLA   No.

GRIF   I'll tell you why. Because you're my secret.

KARLA   Right.

GRIF   Am I your secret?

KARLA   You bet.

GRIF   No, really. Have you ever told anyone about
          me?

KARLA   I don't know.

GRIF   Come on!

KARLA   I don't remember!

GRIF   Nobody outside of camp knows about you. They
          wouldn't get it. My Grandmother would freak.

KARLA   Why?

GRIF   Because! You're odd.

KARLA   Gee, thanks.

                  Pause.

GRIF   Will you still love me again next year, Karla?

KARLA   Sure.

                  GRIF reaches back and holds on to KARLA's hand.

GRIF   I love you, Karla.

KARLA   I love you too, Grif.

GRIF   I love you like a friend, you know?

KARLA   Me too. Like a friend.

GRIF   You love me more than that, don't you?

                  GRIF turns to KARLA.

              Don't you? Don't you love me more than that?

KARLA   What do you mean?

GRIF   Yes you do. Tell me. How do you love me?

KARLA   (*melodramatic*) Let me count the ways!

GRIF   (*laughs*) You're so funny. I love you because you're funny.

                  Pause.

              Why do you love me?

KARLA   I don't know. I just ... love you, that's all.

                  GRIF gently strokes KARLA's leg.

GRIF   Karla?

KARLA   What?

GRIF   You want to be my girlfriend?

KARLA   ... what...?

            GRIF caresses KARLA's face.

GRIF   You want to be my lover?

            KARLA moves away from her.

KARLA   Stop it, Grif.

GRIF   Come on. It's our last night.

            KARLA rises.

KARLA   Go to sleep.

GRIF   I don't want to go to sleep. I wanna ... you
            know.

KARLA   Grif. You're doing this because there's no guys
            around.

GRIF   I'm doing it because I want to.
            With you.
            What do you want to do?

KARLA   This is me, Grif. Karla? A girl?

GRIF   I know...

            GRIF gently kisses KARLA. Pause.

KARLA   Grif. I love you. I really do love you.

GRIF   I love you too, Karla.

            *They kiss again. GRIF leads KARLA down
            and pulls the sleeping bags over them.*

Danny's Place.
DANNY stands wearing a clown nose and holding a bunch of balloons.

DANNY   Hey, Karla! Why are lesbian's houses so strong?
Because they use tongue-in-groove construction!
Ha ha ha ha ha ha!

Did you hear the one about the Dutch lesbian?
She put her finger in the dyke!
Ho ho ho ho ho!

Hey! Why don't lesbians become alcoholics?
Because they know how to hold their "licker".
Ha ha ha ha Ho ho ho ho He he he he!

His manic laughter turns to painful crying.

The Cabin.
It is morning.
KARLA is lying beside GRIF, watching her sleep. The mess-hall bell sounds. KARLA takes a lock of GRIF's hair as before.

KARLA   Grif.

GRIF moans.

The bell.

GRIF   Huh?

KARLA   Grif.

GRIF slowly wakes and tries to sit up.

Good morning.

GRIF moans and holds her head. KARLA reaches out to stroke her head.

KARLA   Poor Grif...

GRIF   Don't.

KARLA   Why?

GRIF   Just don't.

> *They begin to dress in awkward silence. GRIF pulls her things on using the sleeping bag to cover herself. GRIF takes off the wrist band and holds it out to KARLA.*

GRIF   Here.

KARLA   It's okay.

GRIF   Take it.

KARLA   Keep it.

GRIF   I can't wear it at home.

> *KARLA takes it and puts it in GRIF's bag.*

KARLA   Then hide it somewhere.

> *Pause.*

GRIF   Can I have my ring?

> *Pause.*

KARLA   Grif...

GRIF   What?

> *Pause.*

         I need my ring back. My grandmother would be really upset.

KARLA   Tell her it fell off when you were swimming.

GRIF   I don't lie to my grandmother.

KARLA You mean you tell her everything?

GRIF I mean I don't say things that aren't true.

Pause.

I want my ring.

KARLA slips the ring off her finger and holds it in her hand. She stares at it.

KARLA Can we see each other? Meet at a mall or something?

GRIF I don't know.

KARLA I really want to see you back home. It's different now. I can't wait until next summer.

GRIF Give me my ring.

KARLA So that's it? We sleep together and then we don't see each other again?

GRIF I didn't say that.

KARLA You wanted to, remember.

GRIF Look, it's no big deal, okay?

KARLA We said we loved each other!

GRIF Jesus, Karla, I was drunk.

KARLA Wait ... you wanted to. You said you wanted to.

GRIF You knew I was drunk.

KARLA You knew what you were doing! You said!

GRIF I was wasted, okay? It doesn't matter!

KARLA It matters to me Grif! IT MATTERS!

GRIF   Keep your voice down, Karla.

KARLA   Why should I! What difference does it make!
            You don't care what you do to people! What
            you do to me!

GRIF   I do so! I just don't want to make a scene about
            it, okay?

KARLA   Maybe I should tell your Grandmother! Maybe
            she should know!

GRIF   Just give me my ring, dyke.

                 This stuns KARLA.

KARLA   What?

GRIF   Well, look at yourself ! The way you dress.
            The way you act so tough. Drink beer. Do
            drugs. A father who breaks your arm. Hang out
            with people called "Stiff"!

KARLA   Stilt!

GRIF   Face it, Karlo, you're a dyke!

KARLA   And you're a SLUT!

                 *GRIF slaps KARLA. KARLA slaps her back.
                 GRIF tries to hit KARLA again, but KARLA
                 restrains her.*

KARLA   Admit it. Admit it! You wanted me!

GRIF   Let go!

KARLA   We made love!

GRIF   I mean it, Karla!

KARLA   Loud and clear so the whole camp can hear!
            KARLA AND GRIF ARE LOVERS!

GRIF   LET GO!

                KARLA releases GRIF.

                You ever do that again, Karla...

KARLA   And what?

GRIF   I'll say you raped me.

KARLA   (*smirks*) Come on...

GRIF   I got really drunk playing caps with Karla.
                She started pushing me around. She pulled off
                my pyjamas, and pinned me down on the floor.
                Then she held her knife to me, and wouldn't
                let me go. She made me lie still on the cabin
                floor while she...

KARLA   Grif...

GRIF   *Without* my consent.

KARLA   No...

GRIF   Against my will!

KARLA   I didn't...

GRIF   Rape, Karla.

KARLA   Grif, you can't—

GRIF   RAPE!

KARLA   You came on to ME! YOU started it!

GRIF   FUCK OFF!

KARLA   And you liked it! You said it was better than
                any of those guys you lay every weekend!

GRIF   BULL SHIT!

KARLA   It was the best! It was wonderful!

GRIF   NO!

          GRIF angrily kicks the pile of sleeping bags.
          KARLA grabs her jack knife from its sticking
          place on the bunk post and holds it
          menacingly at GRIF, blocking her exit. Her
          hand shakes.

GRIF   What are you doing?

KARLA   I love you.
          Ever since we were ten years old in Cabin
          Eight, I've loved you.
          From the first time you chose me for your
          swimming buddy, and we had to hold hands in
          the water and yell: "BUDDIES!"
          You were my friend. MINE!

          Don't do this. Don't walk out like this. It's
          okay, you know? We don't have to do it again.
          We don't have to DO anything. But don't ...
          please ... don't go.

GRIF   Let me out!

KARLA   Mother may I.

GRIF   Get lost, Karla.

KARLA   Say you love me.

GRIF   Let me out.

KARLA   Say it!

GRIF   I hate your guts.

KARLA   No you don't, Grif...

GRIF   You hear me, Karla? You make me sick! I
          HATE YOU!

> *GRIF kicks KARLA in the stomach. KARLA buckles over and drops the knife. GRIF runs out the door.*

KARLA   GRIF!

Grif...

> *KARLA holds herself, crying. DANNY rushes over to KARLA as if she were a little girl. He holds her face up and wipes away her tears as he sings, comforting her.*

DANNY   You are my sunshine. My only sunshine.

> *He picks up her knife, puts the blade in and hands it back to her.*

You make me happy, when skies are grey.

> *He helps her up and wipes the dirt from her knees.*

You'll never know dear, how much I love you.

> *He gives her a final hug before leaving the stage.*

Oh, please don't take my sunshine away.

> **The Apartment.**
> *GRIF is sitting on the apartment couch as from previous apartment scene, but the light from the TV is as firelight.*
>
> *She gently sings the 'last night of camp' song — "I Wanna Linger". KARLA moves with the same emotion from Danny's song to GRIF's song. She sits behind GRIF on the back of the couch holding GRIF closely, who is relaxed and leaning back against her, gazing into the fire.*

GRIF   mmm mmmm ... I wanna linger ... mmm mmm...
            a little longer ... mmm mmm ... a little longer
            here with you ... mmm mmm ... It's such a
            perfect night ... mmm mmm ... It doesn't seem
            quite right ... mmm mmm ... that this should
            be my last with you ... mmm mmm ... And as
            the years go by ... mmm mmm ... I will
            remember why ... mmmm mmm ... I wanna
            linger here with you...

            *LIGHTS snap immediately to present, as keys
            are heard fumbling in the door.*

            GRIF stands, arranging herself.

KARLA   How quaint! I finally get to meet the man
            with the key.

GRIF   Karla...

KARLA   And the million dollar answer to the question
            ... How really big is he?

            *Enter KATHY, with briefcase. A smartly
            dressed, attractive, professional, confident
            woman. KARLA remains sitting on the back
            of the couch.*

KATHY   Jan?

GRIF   Hi.

KATHY   Hi. You're home.

            KATHY kisses GRIF.

GRIF   Yeah... I... uh... This is Karla.

            KATHY offers to shake hands.

KATHY   Karla.

GRIF   Kathy Westbury.

KARLA   Kathy.

KATHY   (*to GRIF*) I waited for an hour...

GRIF   Oh... I'm... uh... Karla just dropped in.

KATHY   Oh...

GRIF   We... went to camp together.

KATHY   Oh, yes. (*beat*) I called...

GRIF   You did?

KATHY   There was no answer.

GRIF   It didn't ring...

KATHY   That's strange.

> *KATHY checks the phone.*

> It's unplugged.

GRIF   Oh...

KATHY   Is everything alright?

GRIF   Yes, fine.

> *KATHY notices the plates.*

KATHY   Oh. You ate?

GRIF   Um. Yes. Karla made a salad.

KARLA   Greek.

KATHY   Well. Oh.

KARLA   Would you like a glass of wine?

> *Pause.*

KATHY   Yes. Please. I can't stay long, though. I have some preparing to do.

            KARLA pours the wine. GRIF tries to speak in confidence to KATHY.

GRIF   Kathy, I'm sorry. It got ... confusing.

KATHY   You could have called the restaurant.

KARLA   What for?

KATHY   Pardon me?

KARLA   What are you preparing for?

KATHY   Oh. A case for Children's Aid.

KARLA   Oh, yeah.

            KATHY hands her the wine.

KATHY   Thank you.

KARLA   Welcome.

KATHY   Do you live in town, Karla?

KARLA   Yup. Always have. Actually, I just inherited my father's house. In Overbrook.

KATHY   Oh. I'm sorry.

KARLA   Hey, no. It's an okay house. Better than paying rent.

            GRIF laughs nervously.

KATHY   Uh huh... So, what do you do, Karla?

KARLA   I'm a sous chef. At the Delta.

KATHY   Really? Well. We'll have to have you prepare us a meal sometime.

GRIF   Karla was on kitchen staff at camp.

KATHY   Oh... right! I remember now. Are you the girl with the knife?

KARLA   Probably.

KATHY   Jan has some funny stories.

KARLA   What stories?

KATHY   Didn't you put a bunch of dead flies in the camp director's soup, or something?

KARLA   Moths.

KATHY   And spread Handi Wrap across the toilet bowls?

KARLA   No, that was Grif.

GRIF   No, that was you.

KARLA   No. You did the Handi Wrap. I did the Vaseline on the seats. (beat) She always did get confused with the details.

KATHY   What did you call her?

KARLA   Pardon?

GRIF   Oh, "Grif."

KATHY   "Grif."

GRIF   It was a .. It was my / nickname

KARLA   (*at the same time*) /It's what I called her.

KATHY   Oh. It's catchy. I like it. "Grif." So you haven't seen each other for a while, then?

GRIF   No, we kind of lost touch.

KARLA   Kinda.

KATHY   It's a shame when that happens, isn't it? I
            used to go on student exchanges. You know,
            live with a family in another country for a
            month or two? It's like you become sisters. So
            close.

            And you swear you'll be best friends forever.
            And write every month. And visit when you're
            adults.

                *KATHY tenderly removes a strand of hair
                from GRIF's face.*

            And then, of course you never do.

KARLA   No.

KATHY   (*to KARLA*) So, you just surprised Jan? Grif?
            Dropping in unannounced?

KARLA   Yes.

GRIF   She looked up my address in the phone book.

KATHY   (*chuckles*) Oh, that's great.

GRIF   Mmm hmm.

KATHY   Oh, Jan... (*to KARLA*) Excuse me. (*to GRIF*) I
            brought the listing I mentioned.

GRIF   Oh, good.

KATHY   Pamela says that if we want to make an offer,
            we have to move quickly. They just turned one
            down for 92,7. She thinks they'll take 93,5. It's
            going to go. We can see it tomorrow.

GRIF   After work?

KATHY   I can make an appointment for four.

GRIF   Okay.

              Pause.

KATHY   You sure?

GRIF   Absolutely.

KATHY   Great. Okay. Well. I guess you have a lot of
              catching up to do.

KARLA   Yup.

KATHY   I should go then.

GRIF   I'll call you in the morning.

KATHY   Okay. Well. It's good to meet you, Karla.

KARLA   Bye, now.

KATHY   Okay. Well. Goodnight.

              KATHY kisses GRIF.

GRIF   Goodnight.

              KATHY exits. Pause.

KARLA   So... Crazy Eights? Scrabble? (*beat*) Spin the
              Bottle?

GRIF   Karla, listen—

KARLA   Hey, I know! How about a rousing game of
              Truth or Dare?

GRIF   No, Karla.

KARLA   Oh, come on, Grif. It was your favourite. Truth.
              Dare. Double Dare. Challenge or repeat?

GRIF   Stop it.

KARLA   Didn't you hear the bitch? We've got a lot of
             catching up to do. I dare you to tell me the
             truth.

GRIF   Not like this.

KARLA   TRUTH!

GRIF   What do you want to know?

KARLA   Kathy!

GRIF   She's my friend.

KARLA   She was your date!

GRIF   She's a good friend.

KARLA   She has a key to your door!

GRIF   She's a very good friend.

             KARLA picks up the listing.

KARLA   And what's this? A co-operative investment?

GRIF   Yes.

KARLA   You're moving in together!

GRIF   Yes. We are.

             Pause.

KARLA   Repeat.

GRIF   You don't need to do this.

KARLA   Repeat!

GRIF   Get the hell out of my house! NOW!

             *KARLA grabs her knife off of the counter and
             holds it threateningly at GRIF.*

KARLA   REPEAT AFTER ME!

GRIF   Karla, think about what you're doing.

KARLA   Shut up! Repeat! "Kathy is my lover."

GRIF   Put the knife down, Karla!

KARLA   KATHY IS MY LOVER!

                     Pause.

GRIF   Yes.

KARLA   SAY IT!

GRIF   Kathy is my lover.

KARLA   Very good. Now. "Karla did not rape me."

GRIF   Let's... just talk. We can talk—

                     KARLA grabs GRIF's top and pulls her close.

KARLA   Karla did not rape me!

GRIF   Karla did not—

KARLA   Look at me!

GRIF   Karla did not rape me.

KARLA   We loved each other.

GRIF   We loved each other.

KARLA   I hurt Karla's feelings very much.

GRIF   I hurt Karla's feelings very much.

KARLA   I am very sorry.

GRIF   I am VERY...!

        KARLA presses the knife to GRIF's throat.

KARLA   Don't... yell.

GRIF   I am very sorry.

        KARLA releases GRIF and straightens her top.

KARLA   There now. Don't you feel better? Now that the truth is out?

        Pause.

Well. What do we do now?

GRIF   You leave.

KARLA   Kiss and make up?

        GRIF picks up the telephone. KARLA cuts the cord with her knife.

Oops.

        GRIF goes for the door. KARLA is faster. She holds the knife out at GRIF.

KARLA   It's time to kiss and make up.

        KARLA moves close to GRIF and strokes her face.

You are so beautiful.

        GRIF recoils from KARLA's touch.

I don't want to hurt you, Grif. I didn't come to hurt you. I only wanted to see you. To ask you.

Three years, I've been wondering, Grif. If I got it wrong. If it was me who started it. If it was the truth. Or if it was the dare.

KARLA   What was it, Grif?

             Pause.

GRIF   It was both.

KARLA   You used me! Used me for the attraction. Like
             a tattoo. And then you just peeled me off, and I
             shrivelled away.

             Why'd you do that? Why did you leave me?

GRIF   I was afraid!

KARLA   Of me?

GRIF   I didn't want you to need me.

             Pause.

KARLA   Well, I don't need you, Grif. I just want you. I
             want you back.

GRIF   No.

KARLA   I was here first!

GRIF   I'm happy with her!

KARLA   You mean you're loyal? You have an ongoing
             relationship? You've slept with her more than
             once?

             How long, Grif? How long have you been
             happy? How long?

GRIF   Eight months.

KARLA   Eight months. Eight months. EXTRA! EXTRA!
             "Grif Remains a One Woman Girl For More
             Than A Week!" This is big news.

GRIF   It's called commitment!

KARLA smirks.

KARLA   So, when did you make the big switch? Eh?
          After me? Or, maybe you lied. Maybe even
          before me.

GRIF   No. After.

KARLA   You could have called. You could have told
          me. "I'm out of the closet." Or maybe you're
          not. Are you?

GRIF   It depends.

KARLA   On what?

GRIF   On where we are.

KARLA   Does your Grandmother know?

GRIF   Not yet. Soon.

          Pause.

KARLA   So, what's she like?

GRIF   What does it matter?

KARLA   'Cause I wanna know why she gets you and I
          don't.

GRIF   It's different. She's more ... she's ... we're...

          *KARLA, in angry exasperation suddenly kicks
          a vase, lamp, chair or similar object.*

KARLA   WHAT!?

          Pause.

GRIF   Gentle.

          KARLA is on the verge of tears.

KARLA   Gentle? I can be gentle.

GRIF   It's more than that. We respect each other. I admire her. She's talented and successful. We fit!

KARLA   I can't get rid of you. Of remembering you. I remember what if felt like to be around you. To be with you. And that night. What it felt like to be touched by you. Your smell. Your skin. Warm. So... soft. Melting.

                   Take me back. Please, take me back.

GRIF   No, Karla.

KARLA   You can break up with Kathy. You want a house? I have a house. We could have fun. Endless fun, Grif. We know how to have fun!

GRIF   I love Kathy.

                   Pause.

                   I love her.

KARLA   Well.
She doesn't love you.
She told me.
She said to tell you it was over. Get lost. Fuck off. You're ugly.

GRIF   Come on, Karla.

KARLA   You're fat. Fat and ugly.

GRIF   Stop it.

KARLA   Fat and ugly and gay. A fat, ugly, gay slut!

                   But, I still love you anyway.

                 KARLA touches GRIF sexually.

KARLA   Now what are we going to do? Hm?

               *GRIF looks directly at KARLA, allowing
               KARLA to continue caressing her.*

               What do you want?

GRIF   I want my ring back.

KARLA   No.

GRIF   My ring, Karla. Now.

KARLA   Finders keepers.

GRIF   You promised to give it back at the end of the
               summer.

KARLA   Where's my wrist band?

GRIF   I threw it out.

KARLA   Then fuck you!

GRIF   I want my ring.

KARLA   It's stuck.

GRIF   It was my mother's!

KARLA   You try.

               GRIF tries. She can't remove it.

GRIF   Take it off!

KARLA   You'll have to cut it off. Here.

               KARLA offers GRIF the knife.

               Come on. Cut me.

               *GRIF looks at the knife. KARLA holds out
               her hand, palm side up.*

KARLA   Cut me!

> *GRIF begins to slowly cut across KARLA's palm.*

KARLA   Deeper!

> *KARLA takes GRIF's hand and forcibly pushes down harder on the knife.*
> *As she cuts, GRIF begins to shake violently, making a strange guttural noise. KARLA inhales sharply, staring all the time into GRIF's face.*
> *After the knife is drawn all the way across the palm, GRIF drops the knife. KARLA begins to bleed.*
>
> *Pause.*

GRIF   (*weakly*) I'm sorry.

KARLA   Pardon me?

GRIF   You're bleeding.

KARLA   So?

GRIF   Well, stop it! Put some pressure on it!

KARLA   No.

GRIF   Clench your fist!

KARLA   No.

GRIF   Jesus Christ!

> *GRIF grabs the tea towel from the kitchen and hands it to KARLA.*

Here, wrap it!

> *KARLA drops it on the floor.*

KARLA   That one's dirty.

> *GRIF runs into the bathroom. KARLA walks*
> *slowly around the couch dripping her blood*
> *purposely on the floor and over the couch; her*
> *hand in a claw-like position.*
> *GRIF emerges with a handful of first-aid*
> *supplies. She stops and stares at what KARLA*
> *is doing.*

GRIF   ...Karla..?

> *Holding her hand in the air, KARLA speaks*
> *with climactic intensity.*

KARLA   I ... AM ... A ... WOLF!

           THIS is MY territory!

> *KARLA wipes her hand across GRIF's breast.*
> *GRIF doesn't move.*

Mine!

> *KARLA presses her hand to GRIF's crotch.*

Mine!

> *KARLA wipes her hand across GRIF's face.*

Mine!

> *GRIF collapses, crying. KARLA takes off the*
> *ring and places it back on GRIF's finger.*
> *KARLA picks up her knife. GRIF sees this*
> *and tries to get up to run. KARLA is quicker*
> *and puts her hand on GRIF's back. GRIF*
> *freezes.*

I'm not going to hurt you.

> *KARLA grabs a large swatch of GRIF's hair and holds the knife to it. She begins to shake. Her aggressive hold of the hair turns into one of admiration, longing and sorrow. She throws the knife aside. She gently puts GRIF's hair back down. She stands.*

I love you.

> *KARLA moves to the door and puts on her jacket. She stands in the doorway. The last line indicates her pain and vulnerability. She is trying for bravado, but it fails.*

But, I liked you better... as a dirty blonde.

> *KARLA walks out leaving the door open. Lights fade on GRIF.*

The End.